# Stages of Cancer Development

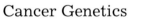

# Stages of Cancer Development

**Paraic A. Kenny, Ph.D.**

Consulting Editor,
Donna M. Bozzone, Ph.D.,
Professor of Biology
Saint Michael's College

CHELSEA HOUSE
PUBLISHERS
An imprint of Infobase Publishing

**THE BIOLOGY OF CANCER: STAGES OF CANCER DEVELOPMENT**

Chelsea House
An imprint of Infobase Publishing
132 West 31st Street
New York NY 10001

ISBN-10: 0-7910-8825-1
ISBN-13: 978-0-7910-8825-8

**Library of Congress Cataloging-in-Publication Data**
Kenny, Paraic.
  Stages of cancer development / Paraic Kenny.
     p. cm. – (Biology of cancer)
  Includes bibliographical references and index.
  ISBN 0-7910-8825-1 (hc : alk. paper)
  1. Cancer–Juvenile literature. I. Title. II. Series.
  RC264.K46 2006
  616.99'4–dc22                                          2006010416

Chelsea House books are available at special discounts when purchased in bulk quantities for businesses, associations, institutions, or sales promotions. Please call our Special Sales Department in New York at (212) 967-8800 or (800) 322-8755.

You can find Chelsea House on the World Wide Web at http://www.chelseahouse.com

Text design by James Scotto-Lavino
Cover design by Ben Peterson
Illustrations by Chris and Elisa Scherer

Printed in the United States of America

Bang EJB 10 9 8 7 6 5 4 3 2 1

This book is printed on acid-free paper.

All links and Web addresses were checked and verified to be correct at the time of publication. Because of the dynamic nature of the Web, some addresses and links may have changed since publication and may no longer be valid.

Gleevec® is a registered trademark of Novartis Pharmaceuticals Corporation; Herceptin® is a registered trademark of Genentech, Inc.; M&M's® is a registered trademark of Mars, Incorporated.

# CONTENTS

◆

# FOREWORD

◆

Approximately 1,500 people die each day of cancer in the United States. Worldwide, more than 8 million new cases are diagnosed each year. In affluent, developed nations such as the United States, around 1 out of 3 people will develop cancer in his or her lifetime. As deaths from infection and malnutrition become less prevalent in developing areas of the world, people live longer and cancer incidence increases to become a leading cause of mortality. Clearly, few people are left untouched by this disease due either to their own illness or that of loved ones. This situation leaves us with many questions: What causes cancer? Can we prevent it? Is there a cure?

Cancer did not originate in the modern world. Evidence of humans afflicted with cancer dates from ancient times. Examinations of bones from skeletons that are more than 3,000 years old reveal structures that appear to be tumors. Records from ancient Egypt, written more than 4,000 years ago, describe breast cancers. Possible cases of bone tumors have been observed in Egyptian mummies that are more than 5,000 years old. It is even possible that our species' ancestors developed cancer. In 1932, Louis Leakey discovered a jawbone, from either *Australopithecus or Homo erectus*, that possessed what appeared to be a tumor. Cancer specialists examined the jawbone and suggested that the tumor was due to Burkitt's lymphoma, a type of cancer that affects the immune system.

It is likely that cancer has been a concern for the human lineage for at least a million years.

Human beings have been searching for ways to treat and cure cancer since ancient times, but cancer is becoming an even greater problem today. Because life expectancy increased dramatically in the twentieth century due to public health successes such as improvements in our ability to prevent and fight infectious disease, more people live long enough to develop cancer. Children and young adults can develop cancer, but the chance of developing the disease increases as a person ages. Now that so many people live longer, cancer incidence has increased dramatically in the population. As a consequence, the prevalence of cancer came to the forefront as a public health concern by the middle of the twentieth century. In 1971 President Richard Nixon signed the National Cancer Act and thus declared "war" on cancer. The National Cancer Act brought cancer research to the forefront and provided funding and a mandate to spur research to the National Cancer Institute. During the years since that action, research laboratories have made significant progress toward understanding cancer. Surprisingly, the most dramatic insights came from learning how normal cells function, and by comparing that to what goes wrong in cancer cells.

Many people think of cancer as a single disease, but it actually comprises more than 1,000 different disorders in normal cell and tissue function. Nevertheless, all cancers have one feature in common: All are diseases of uncontrolled cell division. Under normal circumstances, the body regulates the production of new cells very precisely. In cancer cells, particular defects in deoxyribonucleic acid, or DNA, lead to breakdowns in the cell communication and growth control normal in healthy cells. Having escaped these controls, cancer cells can become invasive and spread to other parts of the body. As a consequence, normal tissue and organ functions may be seriously disrupted. Ultimately, cancer can be fatal.

Even though cancer is a serious disease, modern research has provided many reasons to feel hopeful about the future of cancer treatment and prevention. First, scientists have learned a great deal about the specific genes involved in cancer. This information paves the way for improved early detection, such as identifying individuals with a genetic predisposition to cancer and monitoring their health to ensure the earliest possible detection. Second, knowledge of both the specific genes involved in cancer and the proteins made by cancer cells has made it possible to develop very specific and effective treatments for certain cancers. For example, childhood leukemia, once almost certainly fatal, now can be treated successfully in the great majority of cases. Similarly, improved understanding of cancer cell proteins led to the development of new anticancer drugs such as Herceptin, which is used to treat certain types of breast tumors. Third, many cancers are preventable. In fact, it is likely that more than 50 percent of cancers would never occur if people avoided smoking, overexposure to sun, a high-fat diet, and a sedentary lifestyle. People have tremendous power to reduce their chances of developing cancer by making good health and lifestyle decisions. Even if treatments become perfect, prevention is still preferable to avoid the anxiety of a diagnosis and the potential pain of treatment.

The books in *The Biology of Cancer* series reveal information about the causes of the disease; the DNA changes that result in tumor formation; ways to prevent, detect, and treat cancer; and detailed accounts of specific types of cancers that occur in particular tissues or organs. Books in this series describe what happens to cells as they lose growth control and how specific cancers affect the body. *The Biology of Cancer* also provides insights into the studies undertaken, the research experiments done, and the scientists involved in the development of the present state of knowledge of this disease. In this way, readers get to see beyond "the facts" and understand more about the process of biomedical research. Finally, the books in *The Biology of Cancer* series provide information to help readers make healthy choices that can reduce the risk of cancer.

Cancer research is at a very exciting crossroads, affording scientists the challenge of scientific problem solving as well as the opportunity to engage in work that is likely to directly benefit people's health and well-being. I hope that the books in this series will help readers learn about cancer. Even more, I hope that these books will capture your interest and awaken your curiosity about cancer so that you ask questions for which scientists presently have no answers. Perhaps some of your questions will inspire you to follow your own path of discovery. If so, I look forward to your joining the community of scientists; after all, there is still a lot of work to be done.

Donna M. Bozzone, Ph.D.
Professor of Biology
Saint Michael's College
Colchester, Vermont

# 1

## CANCER: A HISTORICAL PERSPECTIVE

**KEY POINTS**

- Cancer is a disorder in which some of the body's cells begin to grow uncontrollably to form a mass called a tumor.

- Tumors may be benign or malignant. Benign tumors are usually not life-threatening.

- Cancer is an ancient disease, which has afflicted us throughout human history.

## WHAT IS CANCER?

Everybody has heard of it. We all know somebody who has had it. We hear about it on TV and read about it in the newspapers. It seems like every month the news is trumpeting a breakthrough that will "cure" cancer in a couple of years. Despite being very common—perhaps one in three of us will develop cancer sometime during our lifetime—cancer remains

11

mysterious to many people. There are numerous misconceptions about what cancer is (and isn't), what causes it (and what doesn't), and what you can (and can't) do to cure yourself. This book sets out to describe some of the aspects of the group of diseases that we call cancer.

Cancer is a disorder of the body's own cells. As an embryo and a growing child, the cells of our bodies divide rapidly. As we get older, this process slows down, and cells usually only divide to replace cells that are damaged or dead. The cells in the body are kept under tight control, so that they do not divide at inappropriate times. However, cells can be damaged in a way that allows them to escape these strict controls. Uncontrolled multiplication of these damaged cells leads to formation of a tumor.

## CANCER IS NOT JUST ONE DISEASE

People talk of cancer as if it were one disease, but the reality is more complicated and more interesting. The body is made up of many different tissues and most of these have the potential to develop one or more types of cancer. You can get tumors of the brain, intestine, breast, prostate, skin, lung—and all of the other organs. You can also get tumors of the blood, such as different leukemias, which circulate around the body. Tumors that form in different organs tend to have unique characteristics and growth rates. They may respond better to some types of treatment than to others.

Instead of being just one disease, cancer is a convenient name for a few hundred diseases, all of which share a fundamental property: loss of normal growth control. We will learn about how cancer cells escape these normal controls and discuss some of the different cancer types. Along the way, we will meet some of the interesting personalities whose research has shaped what we know of cancer today.

## CANCER IS AN ANCIENT DISEASE

Cancer has been with us for all of recorded history. Ever since humans learned to write, they have been noting the incidence of this disease. Some of the earliest descriptions of cancer are found on papyrus scrolls from ancient Egypt almost 4,000 years ago. The papyrus describes a series of different tumors, including breast cancer. The ancients did not understand what caused cancer, but they recognized that it was a commonly fatal disease.

The ancient Egyptians generally believed that cancer was caused by the gods. It was the Greeks, followed by the Romans, who began the systematic study of cancer. The term *cancer* was first coined by the Greek physician Hippocrates (460–370 B.C.). To Hippocrates (Figure 1.1), a tumor reminded him of a crab, with a central body and extensions at the edges where the cancer invades and spreads. He called this disease *carcinoma* after the Greek word for crab. Hippocrates believed that the body was composed of four liquids, or humors: blood, phlegm, yellow bile, and black bile. Cancer was believed to be caused by an excess of black bile. The teachings of Hippocrates were incorporated and extended by the influential Roman physician Galen (129–199 A.D.), and these ideas were accepted until the Renaissance burgeoned in Europe, more than 1,500 years later.

The Renaissance in Europe was a vibrant period of artistic, cultural, social, and scientific change. In the previous 1,500 years, there were few advances in medical knowledge. There had been strict prohibitions against dissecting bodies after death, for example. Up to this period, the beliefs of the ancients held sway. Most doctors believed in Galen's idea that the blood was pumped by the lungs and was continuously consumed by the organs of the body. The great English physician William Harvey (1578–1657) discovered in 1628 that it was the heart that

**Figure 1.1** The Greek physician Hippocrates coined the word *cancer. (NLM)*

pumped the blood and, instead of being consumed by the organs, the blood was, in fact, circulated around the body.

Giovanni Morgagni (1682–1771) of Padua, Italy, is known as the father of pathology. He spent much of his pioneering career studying bodies, trying to determine the cause of death. He is largely responsible for the introduction of the autopsy in modern medicine. At a time when all manner of treatments were suggested for cancer, Morgagni was convinced that surgery was the only option. In many respects, Morgagni was succeeded by Rudolf Virchow (1821–902) in the nineteenth century, who took advantage of the latest developments in microscopy to take the study of cancer down to the level of the individual cells. His famous law *Omnis cellula e cellula* ("Every cell originates from another cell") provided a central plank in the study of this disease of rogue cells.

## EPIDEMIOLOGY OF CANCER: UNDERSTANDING THE CAUSES

Epidemiology is the study of the patterns, causes, and control of diseases in groups of people. Ever since cancer was recognized as a disease thousands of years ago, people have wondered about its causes. Some great leaps forward in our understanding were made during the eighteenth century in Europe. Bernardino Ramazzini (1633–1714) of Italy observed that nuns almost never developed cancer of the cervix, while they developed more cases of breast cancer than women in the rest of the population. This observation suggested to Ramazzini that sexual and reproductive factors might contribute to the incidence of these diseases. We now understand that sexually transmitted infections (human papillomavirus [HPV]) are a risk factor for cervical cancer and that pregnancy reduces the risk of breast cancer. Here we see an example of how simple observations of large populations can give insight into the complex mechanisms involved in tumor formation.

Another big advance was made in London by Percival Pott (1714–1788) (Figure 1.2), who noticed that chimney sweeps—men and boys who climbed inside the chimneys to clean them—developed

**Figure 1.2** Percival Pott made a big advance in our understanding of cancer when he postulated that chemicals in soot caused cancer in London's chimney sweeps. (*National Library of Medicine/U.S. National Institutes of Health*)

cancer of the scrotum at much higher frequencies than other workers. He found that because the boys went naked to fit in the chimneys, the black coal soot collected against the skin of the scrotum. He postulated that chemicals in the soot could cause cancer and this was later demonstrated experimentally by Katsusaburo Yamagiwa (1863-1930) and Koichi Ichikawa (1888–1948) in 1915 by painting coal tar onto the ears of rabbits.

Smoking is among the leading preventable causes of cancer. For much of the twentieth century, this habit was very popular, even being promoted with doctors in advertisements. The prestigious *Journal of the American Medical Association* even carried advertisements from tobacco companies featuring slogans such as "More doctors smoke Camels than any other cigarette." During the 1930s, cases of lung cancer began to increase. This disease, previously very rare, began its dramatic rise around 20 years after smoking first became popular. Two British physicians, Richard Doll (1912–2005) (Figure 1.3) and Bradford Hill (1897–1991), set out to investigate the cause of this unprecedented increase. They interviewed many patients and investigated many potential causes, such as environmental pollution and the increased use of tar on roads. They published their results in 1950. Of the 649 lung cancer patients interviewed by Doll and Hill, only two were nonsmokers. This surprising finding suggested very strongly that smoking was the primary cause of lung cancer. After obtaining these impressive preliminary results, Doll and Hill went on to survey 55,000 doctors in the following years. They began publishing their results in the *British Medical Journal* in 1954. Using this number of patients, they were able to authoritatively demonstrate an unequivocal link between tobacco consumption and death from lung cancer.

**Figure 1.3** Richard Doll was one of the first people to demonstrate a link between tobacco consumption and death from lung cancer. *(AP)*

In the second half of the twentieth century, the genetic causes of cancer began to be understood. We will explore these causes in detail in the next few chapters.

## WHAT IS A TUMOR?

The word *tumor* comes from the Latin word for "a swelling." A tumor is a mass of cells, all of which originate from one mutant cell. Here, *mutant* refers to a cell that has undergone changes in its **DNA** (deoxyribonucleic acid), its genetic blueprint. The mutant cell has lost the ability to regulate its own proliferation and has begun to grow out of control. After many cell divisions, and usually after accumulating several more mutations, this cell can give rise to a tumor. We will learn more about mutations and loss of growth control in Chapters 2 and 3.

Like all tissues, tumors need food and oxygen, so they contain many blood vessels to transport these nutrients. In Chapter 4, we will learn about angiogenesis, the process by which the tumor tricks the body into providing it with a blood supply. Usually there are many cells from the immune system present in the tumor. Other cells, called *fibroblasts*, are an important part of the tumor **stroma**, the connective tissue framework that gives the tumor structural support.

## BENIGN AND MALIGNANT TUMORS

Tumors start from one cell, which begins to divide uncontrollably. At this point, the tumor can be considered benign. It is usually very small and closely confined to its origin. **Benign** tumors are usually not life-threatening. As tumors acquire more mutations, they can become more aggressive. They can start to digest the **basement membrane**, a dense protein network that surrounds sheets of normal and tumor cells. Because the basement membrane keeps tumor cells constrained, its destruction can allow tumor cells to begin to invade areas away from the site of origin. Chapter 5 describes the different stages of a tumor's progression. At this stage, the tumor is considered **malignant**. Once a tumor becomes invasive and starts to spread from its site of origin, it becomes a real and serious threat to the life of the person. This process is called **metastasis**, and is discussed in detail in Chapter 6.

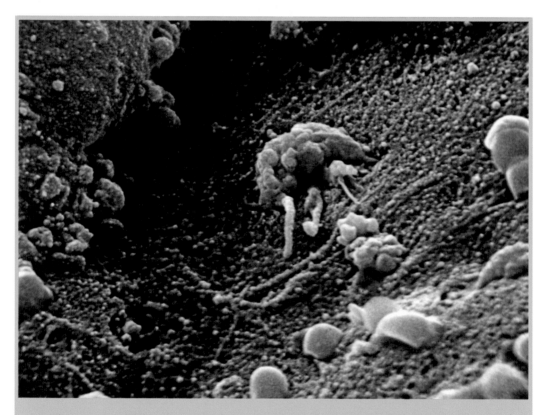

**Figure 1.4** Initial protrusion of melanoma cell process through basement membrane. (*Biophoto Associates/Photo Researchers, Inc.*)

Cancer cells that invade the normal tissue surrounding the tumor can spread to distant parts of the body, either through the lymphatic circulation (a system that produces and transports lymph fluid as a major component of the human immune system), or through the bloodstream. For example, tumor cells from breast cancer can end up finding their way to the brain, bone, or liver, or to all three. When the tumor cells arrive at these distant locations, they colonize the organ and begin to divide all over again. In this way, tumors can spread away from the site of origin and infest many different organs.

It is important to realize that metastatic cancer cells in distant organs still have the characteristics of their tissue of origin. Breast cancer that spreads to the brain is still breast cancer—it just happens to be growing in the brain. It still has many of the same characteristics of the tumor from which it spread (the primary tumor) in the breast and can often be treated in the same way.

Chapters 7 and 8 describe the patient's cancer experience from detection and diagnosis through the various treatment options. For much of human history, there was little chance of recovering from most cancers, but now much progress has been made and complete cures are now possible in a few cancers. For other cancers, the prognosis is not yet as good. Chapter 9 discusses what happens when the cancer comes back after surgery, and will explore some of the issues faced by patients with advanced terminal disease.

In the last chapter, we will assess where cancer research stands today and some of its successes and failures. The last few years have led to some very exciting advances in our understanding of cancer but much more work remains to be done. We hope that cancer research will improve the lives of cancer patients in the not-so-distant future.

## ◆ CANCER VOCABULARY

The names given to tumors can seem complex and confusing. Tumors are named for the cell type of origin. In most cases, the prefix describes the type of tissue in which the tumor is located, while the suffix indicates which of the original germ layers gave rise to the original mutated cell. For example, an *adenocarcinoma* is a malignant tumor arising from an epithelial gland such as the breast, and an *osteosarcoma* is a malignant tumor arising in the bone.

**Prefixes**

*adeno-* means gland

*chondro-* means cartilage

*hemangio-* means blood vessels

*hepato-* means liver

*lympho-* means white blood cells

*melano-* means pigment cell

*myelo-* means bone marrow

*myo-* means muscle

*neuro-* means nerve

*osteo-* means bone

*retino-* means eye

**Suffixes**

*-blastoma* means of embryonic origin

*-carcinoma* means of epithelial origin

*-sarcoma* means of connective tissue origin

## SUMMARY

Tumors arise from the uncontrolled growth of cells that have sustained mutations in their DNA. Most of the tissues in the body can develop tumors, some benign, some malignant. We have learned much about the causes of cancer from epidemiology, the study of disease within large populations. Smoking, which causes lung cancer, is the leading single cause of preventable cancer deaths. Advances in understanding and treating cancer, which is actually 200 hundred different diseases, have made today's expertise possible.

# 2
## ONCOGENES

**KEY POINTS**

- Changes in the sequence of a gene, called mutations, cause the production of altered proteins. If these altered proteins regulate the rate of cell division, cancer can result.

- Mutations can be caused by environmental factors, such as smoking or radiation, or simply by mistakes during cell division in DNA copying.

- Cancer-causing mutations often affect the rate at which cell division occurs. The rate of cell division is controlled by the cell cycle.

## GENES AND DNA

DNA is the genetic material. The nucleus of every cell in our bodies contains 23 pairs of **chromosomes** (except sperm and egg cells, which contain just a single set of 23). Altogether these chromosomes contain around 30,000 genes. The full sequence of all of these genes, the human genome, has been determined, and information is available on the Internet (see the British nonprofit educational site at Human Genome, http://genome.wellcome.ac.uk).

DNA is made up of a seemingly monotonous sequence of four **bases** (also known as nucleotides): adenine (A), cytosine (C), guanine (G), and thymine (T). These bases are held together by hydrogen bonds in a double helix structure. In fact, for a long time after its discovery in 1869, DNA was considered too boring and monotonous to be the genetic material. The detailed structural analysis of DNA convinced researchers that it was indeed the material of inheritance.

Genes are made of DNA and can be composed of anywhere from 10,000 to a couple of million bases in length. Each gene can be transcribed by DNA-processing enzymes into an **RNA** (ribonucleic acid) copy. This copy is then read, three bases at a time, and translated into a string of amino acids called a **protein**. These proteins, in turn, control all aspects of the behavior of the body, including the organization of cells, the organization of tissues, and the interaction between tissues.

## MUTATION

Sometimes changes can occur in the DNA sequence. A **mutation** is a change in one of the bases—for example, an A may be mistakenly changed to a C, T, or G. Changing the sequence of a gene will result in a change in the sequence of the encoded protein. Because proteins need to have the correct sequence to work properly, even small changes can have large consequences.

Gene mutations can happen during the normal copying of DNA that occurs during cell division. DNA mutations occur more commonly as a result of mutagens, substances that damage DNA and modify its structure. Radiation is an example of an environmental mutagen. People who are exposed to nuclear fallout, for example, from a power plant accident, have been exposed to large amounts of high-energy radiation. This radiation can damage the DNA of the cells and cause many mutations. Another example of a mutagenic material is cigarette smoke. One compound in cigarette smoke, benzopyrene, binds directly to DNA, modifying its structure.

## CANCER: A DISEASE OF UNCONTROLLED CELL DIVISION

In multicellular organisms, like plants and humans, **cell division** is very tightly controlled. All of the specialized cells in tissues divide only when necessary, usually in response to a signal from its neighbors that says a replacement is necessary. In some tissues, such as the intestine, the rate of cell division is very rapid. The intestine is quite a hostile environment, and the layer of cells lining the intestine (the colonic **epithelium**) replaces itself every couple of days. The dead cells slough off and exit the body in solid wastes or feces. The skin is another organ which turns over fairly quickly. Other organs, like the liver, don't tend to have high rates of cell division, but if half of your liver is removed during an operation, the remainder will grow back to almost its original size in just one week. Yet other cells, such as nerve and muscle cells, do not divide in the adult.

The rate of cell division is controlled by the **cell cycle**. This is a strictly regulated, ordered series of events in which the chromosomes are duplicated and distributed to two identical "daughter" cells. The cell cycle is controlled by a large group of interacting proteins called cyclins and CDKs (cyclin-dependent kinases), which act in concert to determine if and when a cell should divide. There are also a number of checkpoints in the cycle. When the cell reaches a checkpoint, it stops to make sure that it has achieved all the necessary objectives for that stage of the cycle. These checkpoints are a series of questions a cell must "ask" itself before it makes the final decision to divide. Questions include: Am I big enough? Have I made a second copy of all my chromosomes? Is my DNA damaged? If the answer to any of these questions is no, the cell will not divide. This prevents cells from dividing when they are damaged and helps protect against cancer.

If the cell cycle controls cell division, what controls the cell cycle? Messages instructing the cell to divide usually come from neighboring cells in the form of a secreted protein signal. These soluble proteins bind to receptor proteins on the surface of the target cells. These receptors act like little antennae, constantly listening for instructions. When a growth factor binds to a receptor, the receptor becomes activated and starts transmitting the signal into the cell. The signal is then passed along a chain of different proteins, from the membrane to the nucleus. At this point, if conditions are right, the cell will commence its progression through the cell cycle, ending in cell division. This process of transmitting a signal from outside the cell, through the cell membrane, to the nucleus is called **signal transduction**. Many of the receptors and intermediate proteins are **kinases**, enzymes specialized in adding phosphate groups ($PO_4^{2-}$) to other proteins.

One way in which cancer can develop is if this signal transduction process goes into overdrive. Mutations in the genes that encode these signaling proteins can make the proteins hyperactive and allow them to signal to the nucleus even in the absence of signals from neighboring cells. This unrestrained signaling can lead to loss of regulation of the cell cycle and then to uncontrolled cell division. In this way, the mutant cell makes more copies of itself and becomes a tumor. All of the proteins in the signal transduction pathway are vulnerable to mutation, although cancers in some tissues seem to prefer some mutations over others, for reasons we don't quite understand. For example, in breast cancer, mutations in a signal receptor protein called *HER2* are common, while in colon cancer, mutations in an intracellular protein called *ras* are common. *Ras* is one of the proteins that conducts signals from *HER2* to the nucleus. Knowing more about the different proteins which are mutated will help scientists design better drugs to treat these tumors.

## VIRUSES AND CANCER

Although relatively few human tumors result from viral infections, at least in the developed world, much of our early knowledge of tumor biology came from the study of cancer-causing viruses. In 1910 Peyton Rous (1879–1970), a young scientist at the Rockefeller Institute, made a startling discovery. He was given a chicken to study that had a large tumor. Rous (Figure 2.1) chopped up the tumor and implanted it in healthy chickens, and showed that the tumor could grow in these new hosts. In a series of exciting experiments, Rous ground up some of the tumor to a messy pulp and passed it through a filter so fine that no tumor cells, not even bacteria, could pass through. Injection of this filtrate into chickens also gave rise to tumors. This experiment provided evidence that a tumor could be transmitted without needing to transplant actual tumor cells. The tiny size of the holes in the filter suggested a virus was responsible. These findings eventually led to the discovery of the virus that bears his name, Rous sarcoma virus. Other researchers showed that tumor viruses also exist in mammals. For example, John Bittner (1904–1961) identified a virus causing mammary tumors in mice.

**Figure 2.1** Peyton Rous helped increase our early knowledge of tumor biology through his experiments with tumors in chickens. (*National Library of Medicine*)

## ♦ CERVICAL CANCER

Human papillomavirus (HPV) is the most common sexually transmitted disease in the world. Up to 75 percent of sexually active women will catch it at some point in their lives. Because it often causes few symptoms, most people are unaware that they have it. Although infection often doesn't cause immediate problems, this virus carries a potentially deadly cargo when it infects the cervix. Two of the viral genes, *E6* and *E7*, can knock out some of the key growth regulatory proteins in cervical cells, leading to deregulated proliferation of cervical cells. Many women in the developed world have routine cervical examinations called *Pap smears* that can identify early precancerous cervical changes that might arise from HPV. It is important to have regular Pap smears as recommended by your physician.

Because HPV is a very common infection and not everybody gets cervical cancer, it is important to consider what the risks are. Almost all women who get cervical cancer are HPV-positive (99.7 percent). However, if a million women are HPV-positive, 100,000 of them will go on to develop precancerous changes in the cervix (a one in 10 chance), which may be detected by a positive Pap smear. Of these, only 8,000 will develop early stage cancer (carcinoma in situ). Not all of these women will develop invasive cervical cancer—this will only happen to around 1,600 of these 8,000 women.

A sexually active woman will most likely catch HPV at some point. At that stage, there is a one in 10 chance of developing precancerous changes, so it is important to have regular Pap smears as recommended by your physician. A positive Pap smear is not a reason to panic—only 8,000 women develop the next stage of cervical cancer for every 100,000 who have a positive Pap smear.

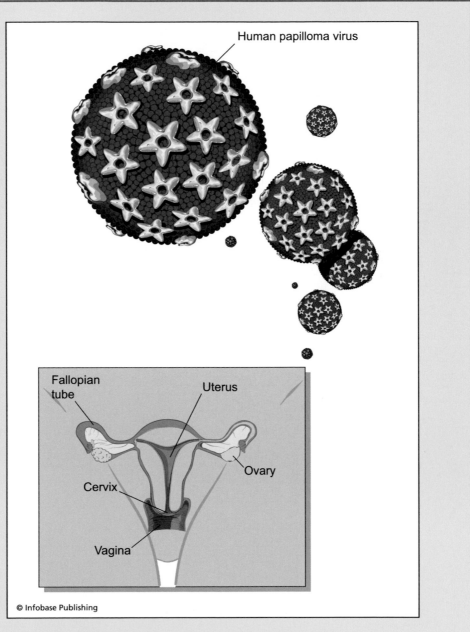

Human papilloma virus

Fallopian
tube

Uterus

Cervix

Ovary

Vagina

© Infobase Publishing

**Figure 2.2**  The female reproductive tract (below) and human papilloma viruses (above).

These findings stimulated huge interest among cancer researchers, and tremendous effort was expended to discover similar viruses which cause cancer in humans. However, after decades of research, it seems

---

### ♦ A HOLLYWOOD DISASTER MOVIE

In 1955 Howard Hughes made a movie called *The Conqueror* in the canyon of Utah. Despite starring John Wayne and Susan Hayward, this movie about the early life of Genghis Khan was a flop at the box office. However, financial failure was the smallest problem. Within a couple of decades of shooting the movie, the majority of the cast and crew—including those in the starring roles—developed cancer, and many of them died.

The movie was filmed near the town of St. George, Utah, downwind of the military atomic bomb test site of Yucca Flats, Nevada. In the two years before the movie was shot, the military tested 11 nuclear bombs at that site, showering the land and people downstream with nuclear fallout. Half of the citizens of St. George developed cancer. When Hughes came to shoot his movie in the desert, his 220-member cast and crew were exposed to massive doses of mutagenic radiation. And if that wasn't bad enough, he shipped 60 tons of the radioactive sand back to Hollywood so he could finish shooting the movie on the set.

Nuclear radiation is very damaging to DNA, causing the strands to break apart in the nucleus. The body's DNA repair program is no match for this massive amount of damage, so unfortunately cancer is often the result.

that most common human cancers do not have a viral component. Some examples of human tumor viruses are listed in Table 2.1 (page 34); also see the Cervical Cancer sidebar.

**Figure 2.3** Troops watch the first U.S. nuclear field exercise conducted on land at Yucca Flats, Nevada, in November 1951. The troops are six miles from the blast.

| TABLE 2.1    HUMAN CANCER VIRUSES | |
|---|---|
| VIRUS | CANCER |
| Epstein-Barr virus | Burkitt's lymphoma |
| Human papillomavirus | Cervical cancer |
| Hepatitis B virus | Liver cancer |
| Human T-cell lymphotropic virus type I | Adult T-cell leukemia |

## CONCEPT OF THE ONCOGENE

**Oncogene**, which means cancer gene, was the name used to describe the genes of a virus, such as Rous sarcoma virus, which cause cancer. In the 1970s it became apparent that these viral oncogenes have cellular counterparts. During the process of viral replication, occasionally viruses will pick up a piece of host DNA (that is, DNA from the genome of the infected cell). If that piece of DNA contains a growth-promoting gene, then a cancer-causing virus can result. The normal copies in the cell are called **proto-oncogenes**, and mainly function to regulate the rate of cell division. If these proto-oncogenes are mutated in our body cells—for example, by smoking, radiation, or a random mistake during cell division—cancer may be the result.

Many dozens of proto-oncogenes have now been identified. Some of the most famous ones are *src*, *ras*, and *HER2*. Each of these genes are important for normal functions, but when mutated they can lead to cancer. The identification of these critical genes and the analysis of how they work have led to several new treatment strategies to inhibit these proteins in tumors. Often the mutations that occur in these genes during cancer progression make the encoded proteins more active, so that they strongly promote cell division.

## SUMMARY

Cancer occurs when genes that control the rate of cell division become activated by mutation. Several of these genes were identified by studying cancer-causing viruses. Even though viruses cause only a small proportion of human cancers, the oncogenes identified in viruses have cellular counterparts that play very important roles in the causation of many cancers.

# 3

## TUMOR SUPPRESSORS

**KEY POINTS**

◆ Tumor suppressor genes protect the cell from becoming cancerous.

◆ Some tumor suppressor genes prevent cancer by slowing down the cell cycle, others by monitoring the DNA for mutations.

◆ Inherited mutations in tumor suppressor genes cause many inherited cancer syndromes.

In the last chapter we learned about proto-oncogenes—genes that normally control the rate of cell division but, when mutated into oncogenes, can lead to the cell becoming cancerous. There is a second major class of "cancer genes" that tend to have the opposite effect as proto-oncogenes. Instead of causing the cell to progress through the cell cycle faster and faster, these genes tend to apply the brakes to the cell cycle, slowing it down. These are called **tumor suppressor genes** and they, too, are often mutated in cancer.

36

Mutations in proto-oncogenes change the amino acid sequence of the protein, causing it to be more active, to be more efficient at doing its job than its normal proto-oncogene counterpart. Mutations in tumor suppressor genes, on the other hand, tend to be of the opposite type. These are mutations that destroy the function of the protein. These proteins, which normally restrict the rate of cell division, can then no longer do this important job. Cancer can be considered a struggle between oncogenes and tumor suppressor genes: The oncogenes are pressing on the gas pedal and, if the tumor suppressor genes fail, the brakes stop working and the cell can quickly get out of control.

Many common familial cancer syndromes are caused by mutations in tumor suppressor genes. Here, every cell in the patient's body already has one mutation in one copy of the tumor suppressor gene. Unlike most people, the person with a familial cancer syndrome has only one working copy of the gene in each cell. As a consequence, such an individual is more vulnerable to cancer as only one more mutation is needed to disable the remaining working copy of that gene.

## THE DISCOVERY OF TUMOR SUPPRESSOR GENES

The concept of tumor suppressor genes was established by the study of a childhood cancer called retinoblastoma, which is a tumor that develops in the eye (*retino-*) of young children. These tumors can occur either **sporadically** (at random in the population) or be inherited in families (**familial**). In the 1970s Alfred Knudson (1922– ) (Figure 3.1), a scientist studying retinoblastoma in children, noticed that those children with a family history of the disease tended to develop tumors at a very young age, often developing tumors in both eyes, sometimes with more than

**Figure 3.1** Alfred Knudson's two-hit hypothesis explained how a tumor suppressor gene might function. (*Courtesy of the Albert and Mary Lasker Foundation*)

one tumor per eye. On the other hand, the children developing retinoblastoma who did not have a family history tended to get only a single tumor that started at an older age.

Knudson analyzed many such cases of sporadic and familial retinoblastoma and came to the conclusion that the patients with the familial form of retinoblastoma were born with one copy of a faulty gene in every cell in the body. In this way, they were predisposed to getting cancer. They only needed to lose the remaining normal copy in one of their billions of cells to get a tumor. In contrast, the children who develop sporadic retinoblastomas were born with two normal copies of the gene in every cell. In order to get a tumor, they needed to get mutations in both copies of the gene in the same cell. The "familial" children are born with one mutational "hit" and need to get only one more hit to get a tumor, while for a sporadic tumor to develop, two hits need to happen in the same cell.

This theory became known as Knudson's two-hit hypothesis. It explained how a tumor suppressor gene might function. It is interesting to consider that Knudson developed his ideas without doing experiments in the lab—he worked by observation and statistical analysis to develop this powerful theory that underlies much of cancer research today. Knudson's two-hit hypothesis was shown to be true 15 years later in 1987, when the gene that causes the retinoblastoma tumor was identified.

Most tumors that occur in the population are sporadic. They arise in people who have no family history of the disease. The proportion of tumors that occur in patients whose parents have had the disease is much smaller, but these are a very valuable group of patients to study in order to understand what causes the disease. After the work of Knudson, there was great interest in studying other cancer syndromes that run in families to try to understand what happens in tumor cells.

## TUMOR SUPPRESSOR GENES IN COLORECTAL CANCER

Another example of a familial cancer is cancer of the colon and rectum. Colorectal cancer is quite common and develops from the cells that line the intestine. These cells have a difficult job to do and are exposed to a lot of noxious compounds every day. Like all tumors, colorectal tumors start out as a small group of renegade cells that stop obeying the normal rules for cell growth control. At this point, the cancer cells are so few in number that they are invisible to the naked eye.

After some time, during which these cells may get more mutations, they become a visible colony of cells called a polyp. The polyp grows bigger, pushing out into the center of the intestine, and can eventually become a life-threatening tumor. Most patients with colorectal cancer get only a single tumor, which if located in time can be removed by a surgeon. Some people, however, have a familial colorectal cancer syndrome. Instead of developing one tumor in their fifties or sixties, this small number of people develop hundreds or thousands of polyps in the wall of their intestines at a young age. Many of these polyps progress to colorectal carcinomas.

This pattern of disease fits Knudson's hypothesis well: The disease runs in families and affected patients get much larger numbers of tumors at a much younger age than is common in the general population. Geneticists have analyzed the DNA among large families that have the syndrome to try to narrow down which of our 30,000 genes causes the problem.

In the case of familial colorectal cancer, this turned out to be a gene called *APC* (adenomatous polyposis coli). Patients with the familial syndrome inherit one faulty copy of *APC* from one of their parents. Every cell in their body contains one working copy and one faulty copy of *APC*. In this way, they are predisposed to developing cancer—they only need to lose the one remaining functioning copy of the gene to get a tumor. People born with two working copies of *APC* (that's most of us) need to lose both working copies in the same cell before we develop a tumor. Getting one mutation in a cell is much more likely than getting two mutations in the same cell, which explains why patients who develop the disease sporadically tend to do so much later in life and to get only one tumor.

## TUMOR SUPPRESSOR GENES IN OTHER CANCERS

Similar genes have been found in several other types of cancer (Table 3.1). A small percentage of breast cancer cases are hereditary, but most are not. Intensive study of families with inherited breast cancer cases

| TABLE 3.1    FAMILIAL (INHERITED) CANCER SYNDROMES | |
| --- | --- |
| SYNDROME | ASSOCIATED GENE |
| Familial adenomatous polyposis (colon) | *APC* |
| Familial retinoblastoma (eye) | *RB1* |
| Familial breast and ovarian cancer | *BRCA1* or *BRCA2* |
| Li-Fraumeni (multiple tissues) | *p53* |
| Basal cell nevus syndrome (skin) | *PTCH1* |
| Neurofibromatosis (nervous system) | *NF1* or *NF2* |

yielded two tumor suppressor genes called *BRCA1* and *BRCA2*. As with familial colorectal cancer and familial retinoblastoma, patients with familial breast cancer inherit one faulty copy of either *BRCA1* or *BRCA2* from one of their parents. These patients with *BRCA1* or *BRCA2* mutations almost all go on to develop breast cancer, and many of them may also develop ovarian cancer.

Perhaps the most famous tumor suppressor gene is *p53*. This gene is so famous it has been on the cover of *Time* magazine. One copy of this gene is mutated in patients born with Li-Fraumeni syndrome. These patients usually go on to develop tumors in several organs. The protein

♦ **GORLIN SYNDROME**

Gorlin syndrome (also called basal cell nevus syndrome) is a familial cancer syndrome in which patients develop hundreds of basal cell carcinomas on their skin. These patients inherit a mutation in a gene called *Patched* from one of their parents. Every cell in their body contains a mutation in one copy of this gene. As we have seen, this is an accident waiting to happen. The ultraviolet light in sunlight can cause damage to DNA. In some cells, the normal copy of Patched gets mutated and a basal cell cancer starts to form. These tumors generally don't spread to other parts of the body, so unlike other cancers they are often not life-threatening. But they can still invade other tissues locally and they need to be surgically removed. For patients who develop hundreds of these tumors, surgery can be very disfiguring. Scientists are now developing skin creams that help prevent tumor development in these patients.

encoded by the *p53* gene functions as a damage sensor. When the cell is damaged—for example, by radiation—*p53* becomes activated and prevents the damaged cell from dividing. Mutated *p53* is dangerous because cells that have been damaged may be allowed to proliferate and possibly become cancerous.

## WHY STUDY INHERITED CANCER SYNDROMES?

We've already seen that only a very small percentage of cancer cases are the result of a familial cancer syndrome. In most cases, cancer develops

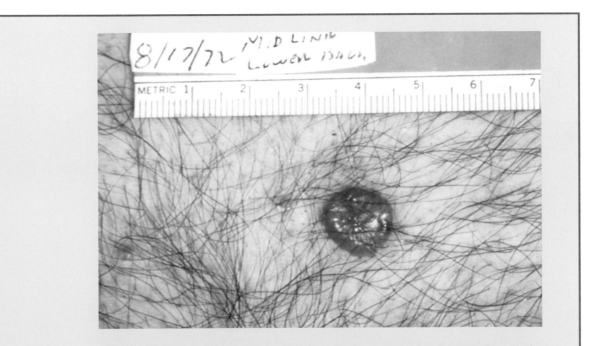

**Figure 3.2** Basal cell carcinoma. Patients who have Gorlin syndrome develop hundreds of basal cell carcinomas on their skin. (*National Cancer Institute/U.S. Institutes*)

because of a combination of poor lifestyle choices (such as smoking and diet), environment, and bad luck. If the familial cases are so much fewer in number than the sporadic cases, then why focus on them? You might think they are an oddity, and study of them to be a distraction from the real business of trying to cure cancer in the rest of the population.

Nothing could be further from the truth. It turns out that the tumor suppressor genes that are mutated in familial cancer syndromes are often the same genes that become mutated as cancer develops sporadically. Studying a small, defined population that develops specific tumors at high frequency is an excellent way to understand the genetics that underlies cancer in the broader population. For example, after *APC* was identified as the colorectal cancer gene in patients with the familial syndrome, analyzing the DNA sequences of sporadic patients showed that this gene was also mutated in their tumors. As another example, inherited Li-Fraumeni syndrome is rare, but mutations in the *p53* gene in the wider population are a very common event in cancer progression. The majority of tumors in tissues throughout the body have mutations in *p53*.

## FUNCTIONS OF TUMOR SUPPRESSOR GENES

Some tumor suppressor genes act to slow down or stop the cell cycle. Without these genes, cells can cycle too rapidly and lead to the inappropriate accumulation of mutant cells. The retinoblastoma gene is a member of this class.

Proteins made by other tumor suppressor genes act as monitors that are constantly watching for problems in the cell's DNA. Perhaps there has been a mutation caused by radiation or some compound in cigarette smoke. Or maybe one of the chromosomes has been broken by radioactive damage. The DNA damage response would then kick in, and the cell would be repaired or, if that is not possible, the cell would die rather than take the risk of becoming a tumor later. The *p53* gene is a member of this class of tumor suppressor gene.

## SUMMARY

In addition to proto-oncogenes, tumor suppressor genes form the second major class of important genes in cancer biology. These genes encode proteins that protect the cell from becoming cancerous. They act to slow down cell division and also prevent cells from dividing if they have sustained mutations in their DNA. If one copy of a tumor suppressor gene is mutated, the remaining copy is usually sufficient to prevent cancer. When both copies are mutated, cancer may result.

# 4

# ANGIOGENESIS

**KEY POINTS**

♦ Like all other cells in the body, tumor cells need oxygen and nutrients to survive and grow.

♦ Tumor cells develop ways of tricking the body into providing them with a blood supply.

♦ It may be possible to treat tumors by blocking the formation of this new blood supply.

All cells in the body have certain needs: They must be supplied with food and oxygen to provide energy and materials for growth and repair. These processes generate many waste products that must, in turn, be removed. These important functions are fulfilled by the **vasculature**, the network of blood circulatory vessels. The heart pumps blood through the arteries, arterioles, and eventually into the capillary beds throughout the tissues of the body. Every cell in the body is no more than 50 to 100 micrometers (the equivalent of around 5-10 cell diameters) away from the blood supply. Without the provision of nutrients and oxygen, the cells would surely starve. A striking example of what can happen when cells don't get nutrients or oxygen can be seen in the results of a heart attack. One of the blood vessels providing oxygen to the cardiac muscle becomes blocked, resulting in death of the muscle fibers and, if not treated very quickly, death of the patient. Similarly, in a stroke, disruption of blood flow to brain cells—either by a clot or rupture of a vessel—quickly results in permanent damage to that region of the brain.

## ANGIOGENESIS IN NORMAL DEVELOPMENT

It is estimated that the human body contains 65,000 miles of blood vessels. The formation of blood vessels during development of an embryo can be divided into two steps. In the first step, vasculogenesis, groups of precursor cells called blood islands differentiate into **hematopoietic stem cells** (which will give rise to each of the types of specialized blood cells). Angioblasts (which will give rise to blood vessels) multiply and differentiate into **endothelial cells**, which form the lining of the blood vessels. These endothelial cells then form tubes called capillaries.

The next step, **angiogenesis**, is the process by which these immature capillaries are remodeled to form the arteries, capillaries, and veins that will supply the tissues with blood throughout the life of the organism. Blood vessels do not originate from a single point—the process of vasculogenesis and angiogenesis happens throughout the embryo and the newly formed blood vessels link up to form the circulatory vasculature. Angiogenesis does not just occur during embryonic development. Whenever new blood vessels are needed—for example, during wound healing or during the cyclic changes in the womb lining during the menstrual cycle—the program of angiogenesis is switched on and new capillaries sprout from nearby blood vessels and bring blood to where it is needed.

## ANGIOGENESIS IN CANCER

Like all the other cells in the body, cancer cells have the same basic requirement for food, oxygen, and waste disposal. In order to grow beyond a certain size, tumors need to figure out a way of persuading the body to provide them with what they need. Without recruiting a blood supply (Figure 4.1), a microscopic tumor will never grow beyond $1/32$ to $5/64$ inches$^3$ (1 to 2 mm$^3$) in size. This limitation of tumor size doesn't mean that the tumor cells are dividing slowly. Often the cells can be dividing just as rapidly at this point as in an advanced tumor, yet the tumor does not seem to get any bigger. How can this be so? As the tumor cells can only survive within a certain short distance from nearby blood vessels, any cell outside of this limit will have insufficient oxygen, a state known as **hypoxia**. These hypoxic cells die in a process called *necrosis*, a combination of starvation and poisoning. In this way, a balance is maintained between tumor cell proliferation and tumor cell death so that the tumor doesn't get any bigger.

## THE ANGIOGENIC SWITCH

Tumor cells are very resourceful and can overcome many challenges presented to them. Eventually, a change occurs in some but not all tumors that allows them to attract blood vessels. This event is known as the angiogenic switch.

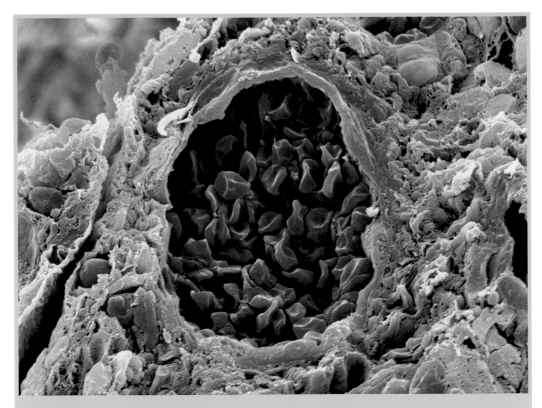

**Figure 4.1** Colon cancer blood supply. Colored scanning electron micrograph (SEM) of a freeze-fractured plane through a blood vessel supplying cancerous colon. Many red blood cells (erthrocytes) fill the blood vessel. Increased blood supply is often seen with cancer, as it is required for the rapid growth of the malignant cells that form a cancer. (*SPL/Photo Researchers, Inc.*)

The formation of new blood vessels during normal embryonic development is regulated by a series of **signaling proteins**. These secreted proteins, which have names like VEGF (vascular endothelial growth factor), bind to endothelial cells (the cells that make the blood vessels) and encourage them to grow. Tumors, needing a blood supply in order to survive and grow ever larger, begin to secrete proteins such as VEGF into

## JUDAH FOLKMAN:
## FOUNDER OF THE ANGIOGENESIS FIELD

In 1961, a young surgeon doing medical research in a U.S. Navy laboratory made a discovery that would ultimately change the way people think about cancer development and treatment. Judah Folkman (1933– ) observed that tumor cells implanted in isolated thyroid glands grew to a tiny size and then stopped. When he isolated these microscopic tumors and implanted them in mice, they grew rapidly. This finding was most puzzling.

However, unlike many scientists, Folkman was a surgeon who had taken tumors from patients and knew how hot and bloody they often were. He realized that the difference in tumor growth between the isolated organs and the mice was due to the growth of blood vessels toward the tumors in

**Figure 4.2** Dr. Judah Folkman's experiments led to the foundation of the field of angiogenesis in cancer research. (*Steve Gilbert/ Studioflex*)

the mice, something that was not possible in his organ cultures. Thus began a decades-long quest to understand the process of angiogenesis. Although his ideas initially met with strong resistance, his persistence led to the foundation of the field of angiogenesis in cancer research. His laboratory went on to identify numerous activators and inhibitors of angiogenesis, and some of these inhibitors have been developed as cancer therapies.

their surrounding environment. Suddenly, the nondividing endothelial cells that form the blood capillaries receive a flood of signals saying "More blood needed over here!" Accordingly, the cells of the capillaries reorganize in order to obey the urgent instruction and begin to sprout new vessels in the direction from which the signals are coming.

The new blood vessels surround the tumor, nourishing it. The tumor can then begin to expand, growing around its blood supply, so that the tumor and its feeding system are intimately linked as the tumor grows. Thus, the tumor co-opts the mechanisms of normal angiogenesis and effectively tricks the body into providing its requirements. Now that its needs for nutrition, oxygen, and waste disposal have been met, the tumor cells can grow and divide beyond their initial limit.

Ninety-five percent of deaths from solid tumors (as opposed to tumors of the blood) result from metastasis—the escape of tumor cells from the primary tumor and their growth and colonization of distant parts of the body. Tumors cells may spread through the blood circulation or **lymphatic system,** a process described in detail in Chapter 6. Thus, in addition to bringing food and oxygen to the tumor, the process of angiogenesis gives tumor cells an escape route to reach other parts of the body.

## BLOCKING TUMOR ANGIOGENESIS

As tumors need new blood vessels and a continued supply of blood to grow, scientists have suggested that blocking this process might be a useful way of targeting tumors. By blocking provision of oxygen and nutrients, tumors might effectively be starved to death or at least made more vulnerable to other treatments. As part of normal development, the body has several ways of switching on angiogenesis, but it also has several ways of suppressing it and switching it off (Table 4.1).

In addition to signaling proteins such as VEGF, which promotes angiogenesis, other proteins can instruct endothelial cells to stop growing. Some examples of these anti-angiogenic proteins include endostatin and tumstatin. There is a balance in the tissues of the body between pro-angiogenic and anti-angiogenic factors. Tumor cells tip this balance in favor of angiogenesis, thus allowing tumors to grow. Scientists hope that by mimicking the action of anti-angiogenic proteins the tumor blood supply could be interrupted, and the growth and spread of the tumor would be stopped.

♦ CANCER AND DOWN'S SYNDROME

A very interesting phenomenon has defied explanation until recently. People with Down's syndrome almost never get cancer. Down's syndrome is a birth defect that results from every cell in the child's body containing three copies of chromosome 21. The extra chromosome 21 results in a series of characteristic **phenotypes**, or specific traits, including slow mental development. As the care for people with Down's syndrome has improved in recent decades, many more are living into their fifties and sixties, the ages where cancer incidence tends to rise. A study of 17,000 people with Down's syndrome who died in the 1980s and 1990s revealed that they suffered from cancer only one-tenth as much as the rest of the population. Why would this group of people experience 10 times less cancer than the rest of the population?

There are several possible answers to this question. For instance, because of their disabilities, these patients often don't work and so are less

## WHY MAKE DRUGS AGAINST BLOOD VESSELS?

Perhaps developing and using drugs to block angiogenesis might not seem like such a good idea. The organs in the body need a blood supply to survive, and attacking the blood vessels in the tumor might be expected to have adverse side effects throughout the body. New cancer drugs act by blocking the formation of new blood vessels (neo-angiogenesis), which will not compromise existing blood vessels because an adult's vasculature serving the organs of the body is sufficiently well

likely to be exposed to carcinogens in the workplace. Often they neither smoke nor drink alcohol, which may explain part of the reduced risk. A very interesting hypothesis is that their extra chromosome 21 contains the gene for endostatin, a potent inhibitor of angiogenesis. People with Down's syndrome have three copies of this gene in every cell instead of the normal two copies. Perhaps they develop the same number of tiny tumors as everybody else, but their extra copy of endostatin prevents the angiogenic switch, which allows microscopic tumors to grow. When scientists have tested the blood of people with Down's syndrome, they found that the concentration of endostatin is about 50 percent higher. Could this be the reason for the reduced incidence of cancer deaths?

Scientists are now testing this hypothesis using genetically engineered mice that, like people with Down's syndrome, make excess endostatin. They find that tumors grow much more slowly in these mice, suggesting that the excess endostatin in people with Down's syndrome might indeed underlie the striking reduction in tumor formation in this population.

| TABLE 4.1    SIGNALING PROTEINS INVOLVED IN ANGIOGENESIS | |
| --- | --- |
| PRO-ANGIOGENIC PROTEINS | ANTI-ANGIOGENIC PROTEINS |
| Vascular Endothelial Growth Factor (VEGF) | Angiostatin |
| Basic Fibroblast Growth Factor (bFGF) | Endostatin |
| Epidermal Growth Factor (EGF) | Tumstatin |
| Transforming Growth Factor-alpha (TGF-α) | Restin |
|  | Thrombospondin |

established. By contrast, tumors need to generate a new blood supply to feed the growing tumor, so by specifically blocking the formation of new blood vessels, tumors might be more effectively targeted. These new blood vessels are good targets because, unlike tumor cells that are genetically unstable and can mutate to become drug-resistant, the blood vessels feeding the tumor are not malignant and cannot mutate to adapt to changing conditions.

More than 60 drugs are now in development to target angiogenesis. Many researchers feel that angiogenesis inhibitors will be best used in combination with existing therapies, such as chemotherapy and radiation therapy. Since the acceptance of the initial studies of Judah Folkman, this exciting field has rapidly expanded and there is considerable hope that it will provide many therapies to help cancer patients.

## ◆ THALIDOMIDE: A GOOD USE FOR A BAD DRUG?

During the 1950s, a drug called *thalidomide* was introduced in Europe to combat morning sickness during pregnancy. Although it was effective against morning sickness, it quickly became apparent that this drug had dire consequences for the children of these mothers. Many babies were born with developmental abnormalities, including stunted limbs and malformed hands and feet. The cause of this outbreak in birth defects was quickly traced to thalidomide and the drug was withdrawn from the market, but not before several thousand unfortunate children were harmed throughout Europe (the drug was not approved for use in the United States).

Up until the 1990s, doctors did not understand how thalidomide wreaked its havoc on the fetus. A scientist working at Harvard Medical School, Robert D'Amato, suspected that the limb malformations might be due to a defect in angiogenesis, as the formation of new blood vessels is critical for normal limb development. Experiments in mice and rabbits demonstrated that this idea was correct, and several trials are now under way in patients to test the usefulness of this drug in human cancer as an angiogenesis inhibitor.

**Figure 4.3** A three-year-old girl, born without arms to a German mother who took the drug thalidomide, uses power-driven artificial arms. (*AP*)

## SUMMARY

Targeting tumor cells in the body requires an understanding of the factors cancer cells need to survive. The supply of oxygen and nutrients and the disposal of waste products are just as important for tumors as they are for healthy tissues. Tumors use the same processes that the body does during normal development to trick nearby blood vessels into sprouting new capillaries to feed the tumor. A number of drugs are now being developed to block this process.

# 5

# STAGES OF CANCER PROGRESSION

**KEY POINTS**

◆ Malignant tumors don't suddenly appear. They arise by slow progression, starting from a normal cell that acquires a mutation and proceeding through several stages before becoming malignant.

◆ Each of these stages can be distinguished by certain characteristics.

◆ Treatment of tumors before they become malignant often leads to a good outcome for a patient.

In Chapters 2 and 3 we learned about some of the genetic alterations—activation of oncogenes and loss of tumor suppressor genes—that can lead to loss of control of proliferation in a tumor cell. In this chapter, we will take a step back from the molecular biology of tumor cells and consider the different changes that take place during the evolution of a tumor cell—from a normal cell to an initially benign growth to a malignant metastatic tumor that threatens the life of a patient.

## EVOLUTION OF THE CANCER CELL

The growth of a tumor can be thought of as an evolutionary process. Our bodies have several controls that restrict abnormal growth, and each of these must be overcome by the cancer cell in the progression toward malignancy.

Malignant tumors contain many genetic alterations, but these don't all happen at once. A tumor begins with a cell that has sustained a single mutation that offers it an advantage over its neighbors, such as the ability to grow more quickly, to become insensitive to growth inhibitory signals, or simply to survive when normal processes of the body attempt to eliminate it. The mutation can be one that activates a proto-oncogene or inactivates a tumor suppressor gene. Next, division of that mutated cell leads to the production of a clone of cells within the tissue. After some time, one cell in this clone may sustain another mutation, which allows it to grow faster than its neighbors that carry only a single mutation. Because the double mutant cell can grow faster, soon its daughters outgrow the cells with only one mutation. This kind of competition, in which there is a selection for mutations that lead to faster growth (or to other things useful for a tumor cell, such as angiogenesis) is what drives the evolutionary changes observed in cancer progression.

Each of these genetic changes leads to a progressive alteration in the appearance and behavior of the tumor cells. These cellular changes can be seen in tissue samples using a microscope. The earliest detectable alteration in tissue structure is **hyperplasia** (excessive growth). Hyperplasia is a precancerous state that might or might not ever become a cancer. It is characterized by an increased number of cells that are still very similar in shape and organization to normal cells. Hyperplasia may or may not result from a cellular mutation. It can also be a response to inflammation in the tissue or to some other stress. For example, the patch of toughened skin (callus) that can build up on your hand when you start to play tennis is a hyperplasia. Obviously, tennis does not cause cancer and the callus will go away with time. Therefore, hyperplasia is not an irreversible state and the tissue can often return to normal without further consequences.

The next stage of cancer development, which can arise from hyperplasia, is called **dysplasia**. The cells have begun to lose the normal orderly arrangement and appearance found in both normal and hyperplastic tissues. Dysplastic cells may divide more rapidly than their hyperplastic precursors, and they also share some of the properties of malignant cells. They often have relatively large and irregularly shaped nuclei, a feature that can aid in a pathologist's diagnosis. Like hyperplasia, dysplasia is an abnormal growth that is not yet cancer. It may return to normal (regress), persist without significant changes, or it may accumulate further changes leading to malignancy.

**Carcinoma in situ** is an advanced state of dysplasia but it is still not a malignant cancer. In carcinoma in situ, the dysplastic cells have expanded and few normal cells remain. Nevertheless, this colony of abnormal cells is still surrounded and constrained by a basement membrane. There are no blood vessels (or lymphatics) inside the carcinoma in situ, as they too are separated from the growth by the basement membrane. Consequently, cells from carcinoma in situ cannot metastasize (spread) to other areas of the body, which is crucial, because if surgery can remove the cancer before it spreads, the chances of recovery are usually very good.

## INVASIVE CANCER

All of the above lesions are benign (Figure 5.1), which means that they are generally not life-threatening. They are distinguished from malignant lesions by lack of invasion into the surrounding tissue. The acquisition of the ability to invade surrounding tissue is the crucial threshold that divides nonmalignant (benign) from malignant tumors. Surgical removal of benign tumors, if they are detected early, is often straightforward and the patient will often make a full recovery.

Once a tumor has become an **invasive cancer**, the patient and doctors are confronted with a range of problems not seen in benign disease. If the cancer has spread to other parts of the body, it becomes very difficult to cure. At this point, it is no longer possible to remove all

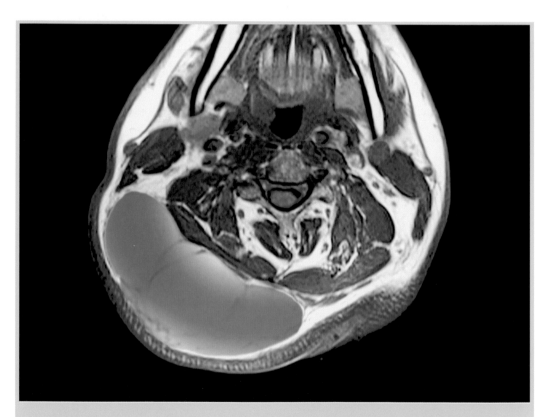

**Figure 5.1** Color enhanced axial MRI showing a benign tumor in the back of the neck (pink). (*Neil Borden/Photo Researchers, Inc.*)

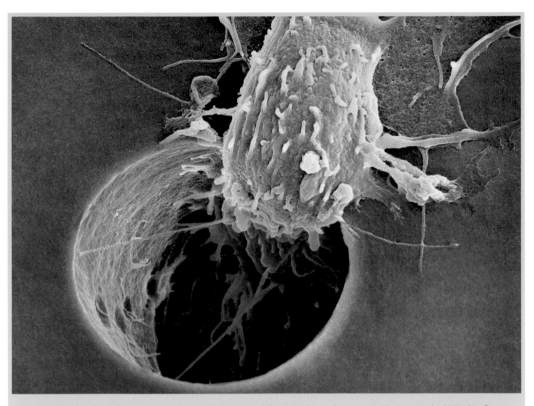

**Figure 5.2** Migrating cancer cell. Colored scanning electron micrograph (SEM) of a squamous cell carcinoma (SCC) cancer cell migrating down a pore in the filter on which it has been cultured. The movement of cancer cells around the body (metastasis) is an important part of a cancer's malignancy. (*A. Weston, S. Gschmeissner, Debra/Photo Researchers, Inc.*)

of the cancer cells by surgery. Even though the primary tumor can be removed, it is impossible to surgically track down and excise all of the tumor cells that may have escaped from the primary site.

Benign tumors are usually smooth around the edges and are separated from nearby normal tissues by the basement membrane. In order to become invasive, this basement membrane, which is made of proteins, must be broken down. Tumor cells produce many enzymes, called **proteases**, which degrade proteins (see "Proteases" box). Production of these enzymes allows the tumor cells to degrade the basement membrane. When the basement membrane is disrupted in this way, there is no longer an effective barrier to keep the cancer cells in place. The cells can then start to migrate out of the tumor. When an invasive tumor is examined under the microscope, it is often irregularly shaped, rather than smooth, at the edges, and it is possible to see the tumor cells migrating away (Figure 5.2) from the primary tumor. Once the basement membrane has been broken down and the tumor cells begin to invade the nearby normal tissues, the cancer is considered malignant and a threat to the life of the patient.

## METASTATIC CANCER

Once a cancer has developed the ability to break down the basement membrane and invade surrounding tissues, it will often begin to spread to other parts of the body. This process is called metastasis. Cells often spread first to nearby **lymph nodes** and then to other parts of the body. Colonies of cancer cells can become established in distant organs and begin to grow. In most cases, it is these colonies, called metastases, which will ultimately cause death from cancer as they disrupt the function of the organs that the body needs to survive. We will learn more about metastasis in the next chapter.

## WHAT PATHOLOGISTS LOOK FOR

A lot can be learned by examining samples from a tumor. A piece of a tumor can be obtained by **biopsy**, an operation that removes a tiny amount of tumor for analysis, or it may be done by examining slices of a whole tumor removed during surgery. This examination is the job of the pathologist, a doctor who specializes in examining tissue and diagnosing disease. When a pathologist examines a tumor, there are a number of important things that are measured.

## Size

If the whole tumor is removed, the size is recorded. Size is an important factor, as large tumors generally have a worse outcome than small tumors.

---

### ◆ PROTEASES

A protease is an enzyme that digests other proteins. It is a very common class of enzyme; there are 650 proteases encoded in the human genome. Each protease digests substrates, or a given set of proteins. Several proteins, such as trypsin and pepsin, are well known for their function in breaking down the proteins we ingest in our food, allowing them to be absorbed by the body. However, proteases have many functions outside of the digestive system.

Proteases inside the cells of the body play important roles in breaking down proteins so that their amino acids can be recycled into new proteins. There are several proteases secreted from the cell surface into the surrounding environment. These proteases play very important roles during development and in processes such as wound healing. In cancer, proteases are often overproduced and these can stimulate the growth of tumor cells, their invasion of surrounding tissues, and metastasis. Several drugs are now in development to target particular proteases with roles in cancer.

## Margins

When a whole tumor is removed during surgery, the pathologist must determine carefully whether all the cancer has been removed from the body. To do this, the pathologist rolls the tumor in ink so that it is all black on the outside. Then several slices of the specimen are examined. If the specimen is surrounded by a layer of normal tissue, stained black by the ink, then it is likely that all the cancer has been removed. If the pathologist finds tumor cells that are black (and therefore at the edge of the specimen), the surgeon may not have removed all of the tumor. In this case, the doctors must decide whether the patient should return for more surgery to remove the remainder of the tumor.

## Grade

**Differentiation** refers to the specialized organization and function of cells. Cells in the organs of the body are found in very typical arrangements and have specific patterns of gene expression. These are the hallmarks of the differentiated state. When tissue becomes disorganized as a tumor forms, the cancer cells may retain or lose certain aspects of the differentiated state. A tumor whose cells closely resemble the tissue of origin is considered well-differentiated, while a tumor whose cells are very disorganized is considered poorly differentiated. From many studies, pathologists have concluded that patients with well-differentiated tumors often have a better prognosis.

Another important reason for studying differentiation occurs when doctors find a metastasis—for example, in a lymph node—but do not know where the primary tumor is. In this case, careful analysis of the tumor cells can give the doctors a very good idea where to look for the primary tumor. By assessing the state of differentiation of the tumor, the

## ◆ HOW MANY OF US WILL REALLY GET CANCER?

It is often quoted that between one in three and one in four of us will get cancer at some point in our lives. Here, *cancer* refers to the disease at the point that it is detected and treated by doctors. There have been some interesting studies performed to check the true incidence of cancer. Doctors examined the organs of a large number of people who had died from other causes (such as accidents or heart disease) to see if they also had signs of cancer. The results show that many more than one in three people have signs of early cancer. Because we know the frequency with which people are diagnosed with each cancer is much less than the numbers of tumors found in these studies, we now realize that many people develop small tumors, mostly carcinoma in situ, which never go on to become a clinical problem.

Even though only 1 percent of men in their sixties are diagnosed with prostate cancer, 40 percent of men at autopsy were found to have small tumors in their prostate glands; while 1 percent of women in their forties are diagnosed with breast cancer, a study of 110 autopsied Danish women found that 39 percent of them had evidence of early breast cancers, often more than one, and often in both breasts. Thyroid cancer is considered quite rare and is only diagnosed in one in every 1,000 people in their fifties and sixties. A Finnish study, which dissected the thyroid glands of 101 cadavers, found that almost all of them had evidence of small thyroid tumors. These studies show that early stage cancers are extremely common but that they rarely progress to life-threatening disease.

pathologist can assign a score, or grade, to each tumor. Well-differentiated tumors have a low grade and poorly differentiated tumors have a
higher grade. Grade 1 tumors are usually slow-growing, while Grade 3
tumors grow much more quickly.

## Stage

Another important measurement is the **stage** of the cancer, sometimes
designated with a number from 0 to Roman numeral IV. The stage takes
into account some important factors, such as the size of the tumor,
whether it has spread to nearby lymph nodes, and whether it has metastasized. Tumors that are larger or that have spread to other parts of the
body have a high stage number; such an advanced tumor has the worst
prognosis.

## SUMMARY

Tumors evolve from normal cells by the acquisition and accumulation
of mutations over time, which leads to progressively disordered tissue
architecture and rapid growth. Tumors are considered benign until they
develop the ability to invade surrounding tissues. At this stage, metastasis
to other parts of the body is a real danger. The pathologist plays a very
important role in examining the tumor and determining the prognosis
of the disease.

# 6

# METASTASIS

**KEY POINTS**

♦ Metastasis is the spread of cancer cells from the site of the primary tumor to other parts of the body.

♦ After a tumor has metastasized, the cancer becomes much more difficult to treat.

♦ Most cancer deaths result from metastasis.

Primary tumors very rarely kill patients. In fact, deaths caused by primary tumors usually only happen when the tumor forms a mass that obstructs the function of a vital organ, such as the brain. In the vast majority of cases, people who die from cancer die as a result of metastases: Secondary tumors that spread from the primary tumor to distant sites. Unlike primary tumors, metastases may be widely disseminated and can often be difficult to find. As a result, they are very difficult to treat by either

67

surgery or radiation. These metastases can disrupt the function of, or even destroy, the organs to which they spread.

Once a primary tumor has become invasive and started to push into the surrounding tissue, metastasis becomes an important concern. A patient with aggressive cancer may end up with many of these secondary cancers spread throughout the body. Often, the process of metastasis begins early in the life of the tumor, so that by the time the patient and doctors realize it is there, the tumor has already begun to shed invasive metastatic cancer cells. Even when the primary tumor is removed by surgery, if cancer cells have already escaped, they may be lurking throughout the body, establishing small secondary tumors that can possibly kill the patient. For this reason, patients are often given chemotherapy after surgical removal of the primary tumor. Doctors assume that the cancer may have spread, so although they can't find any of these metastatic cells, they treat the patient with chemotherapy in an attempt to kill any cells that may have escaped before surgery.

Because established metastatic tumors pose such a grave threat to the life of the patient, the question of whether or not a cancer has metastasized is a key one for doctors and pathologists. Tumors that might otherwise be given a good prognosis, perhaps because they are small upon discovery, are automatically given a high stage score if metastasis has occurred.

Cancer cells that have spread to distant sites still possess many of the characteristics of the primary tumor. So, breast cancer cells growing at distant sites do not become bone cancer or lung cancer—they remain breast cancer. The origin and identity of the tumor cells has important implications for treatment, because cancers of different tissue origins are often sensitive to different drugs. Therefore, a patient with a breast cancer metastasis to the lung will still be treated as a breast cancer patient and not a lung cancer patient.

## HOW DOES CANCER SPREAD?

We have already learned a lot about how primary tumors form and the processes that are involved. We know that tumors generate their own blood supply in the process of angiogenesis. Unlike the normal blood vessels in the body, blood vessels in tumors tend to be leaky, thus providing an access route for tumor cells to escape into the circulation and spread around the body.

The other major circulatory system in the body is the lymphatic system (Figure 6.1). The tissues of the body are bathed in interstitial fluid, which leaks from the blood vessels. This interstitial fluid is collected by the lymphatic circulation and transported as lymph through a system of vessels, channels, and nodes and eventually returned to the blood circulation. Lymph is a pale yellow fluid. The lymphatic system also plays a role in the immune system, with many white blood cells resident in the lymph nodes. These white blood cells form an important part of the body's defense against invading bacteria and viruses. If you have ever had a bad cold, you may have noticed some swelling in your neck—this is an inflamed lymph node reacting to the infection. Each of the tissues of the body is served, or drained, by a different set of lymph nodes. The fluid accumulating in that tissue is taken up, filtered through the nodes, and returned to the venous circulation. If there is an invasive tumor in the tissue, the spreading tumor cells can travel through the lymph vessels to the lymph node, where they can establish metastatic colonies.

The blood circulatory system is composed of arteries, veins, and capillaries. Capillaries are very small vessels with thin walls that supply food and oxygen to individual cells in each of the organs. Each of our organs contains a dense network of narrow capillaries, called the *vascular bed*. Red blood cells are also small and can squeeze through these narrow passages. In contrast, tumor cells are often much larger than red blood

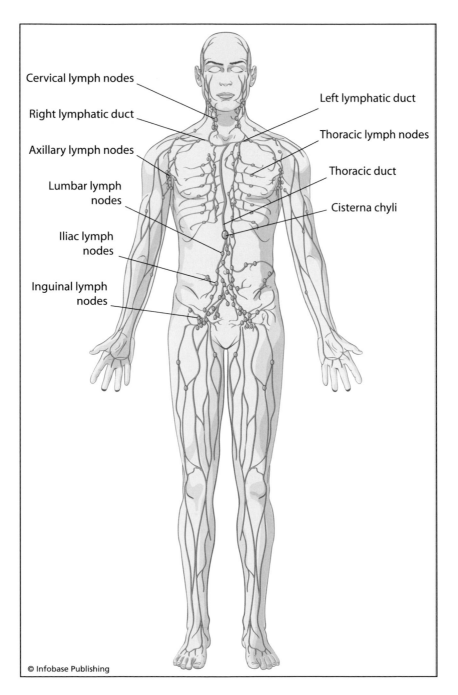

**Figure 6.1** The lymphatic system.

cells. If tumor cells spread via the blood, they often get stuck in the capillaries of the first organ they meet. The tumor cells may then start to divide and invade that organ, starting a metastatic cancer colony.

Because the blood circulation follows an orderly route through the body, tumors in particular organs tend to metastasize (at least at first) in an orderly manner. If they spread via the blood, they often tend to spread first to the organ that is "downstream" in the blood flow. Because of the way the body is arranged, the first vascular bed most tumor cells will encounter upon entering the bloodstream is in the lungs. The intestines are an exception to this rule, as blood from here first travels to the liver.

While spreading to downstream organs is a general rule that applies to many cases, metastatic cancer cells are often found in additional organs. Prostate cancer is an excellent example. Cells that enter the bloodstream from a prostate tumor most often end up forming metastasis in the bone despite the fact that they must pass through the lungs on their way to the bone. There is something about the lung that prostate cancer cells find unfavorable, choosing instead to continue their journey until they find a more hospitable organ. In 1899, Dr. Stephen Paget (1855–1926) proposed his famous "seed and soil" hypothesis. He considered that cancer cells were

| TABLE 6.1 COMMON SITES OF METASTASIS | |
|---|---|
| SITE OF PRIMARY TUMOR | COMMON SITES OF METASTASIS |
| Prostate | Bone |
| Breast | Bone (also liver, brain, and lung) |
| Colon | Liver |
| Lung | Brain |

like seeds and would only grow when they found a suitable site, "the soil." The soil here represents different factors in the microenvironment of the distant organ that are conducive to growth of tumor cells from other organs. Certain organs are better for some cancer cells than for others (Table 6.1).

---

### ♦ LANCE ARMSTRONG: CANCER SURVIVOR

Many athletes aspire to great feats, but few achieve them. Winning the Tour de France is a grueling challenge—a 2,000-mile bike race through the French countryside and mountains over three weeks. American cyclist Lance Armstrong first won this race in 1999, and then won six more times in a row since then. This amazing achievement is even more astonishing when you consider that Lance Armstrong was diagnosed with metastatic testicular cancer in 1996. After feeling some pain in a testicle and coughing up some blood, Lance underwent an ultrasound examination, which revealed a testicular tumor. Chest X rays and a brain scan revealed that the cancer had already spread to his lungs and brain.

Luckily testicular cancer has one of the highest cure rates. Up to 95 percent of patients can be cured with cisplatin chemotherapy. The cancerous testicle was removed and doctors also operated to remove two metastases in the brain. Four treatment cycles of the chemotherapy cleared up the remaining metastases and Lance was soon back in training. He went on to start the Lance Armstrong Foundation (http://www.livestrong.org), which provides support to cancer patients and to cancer researchers.

It is also important to make the distinction between cancer cells spreading into the circulation (dissemination) and metastasis. Large tumors may shed millions of cancer cells per hour into the circulation, but relatively few metastatic cancers result, showing that metastasis

**Figure 6.2** Lance Armstong on the podium after winning the third stage of the 55th Criterium du Dauphine Libere cycling race in southeastern France in June 2003. (*Patrick Gardin/Associated Press*)

is actually quite a rare event. It suggests that the tumor cells have to overcome significant hurdles to survive and divide at distant sites. In order to get into the bloodstream, the cells first need to have developed the ability to invade blood vessel walls. Once in the blood, they are faced with an environment totally different from that which they were used to in their tissue of origin. First, blood is a liquid and, like other cells, cancer cells are used to having other cells and a basement membrane to which they stick. This adhesion provides crucial survival signals to noncancer

## ◆ ACCIDENTAL CANCER TRANSPLANTS

In the past, cancer was often considered to be an infectious disease and it was believed that you could catch cancer from an "infected" person. We now know that, while some cancers such as cervical cancer are associated with viral infection, most cancers don't spread from person to person. Sometimes, however, patients needing an organ transplant such as a liver, lung, or kidney might receive an organ that contains metastatic cancer cells. In these cases, the donor will have had cancer, but it may have been in an early stage and not detected by the doctors at time of death. Such an event happens very rarely.

In a case in Germany, the organs of a donor were implanted in a number of patients. After the surgery, tests revealed the presence of metastatic pancreatic cancer in the donor. A patient who had received the donor's liver was re-transplanted with a new liver within 24 hours. The kidney recipient decided against additional surgery, and the metastases spread from the kidney after nine months and that patient died 15

cells and cells will usually die quickly if they are detached from the basement membrane or other cells. This cell adhesion dependency represents an important safeguard that our bodies have developed to try to limit the spread of cancer cells in the circulation.

If the cancer cell can manage to survive in the bloodstream long enough to reach another organ, it is then faced with the difficulties of leaving the circulation and entering the tissue. This entry can happen in a number of ways. Often tumor cells are relatively large (compared to the

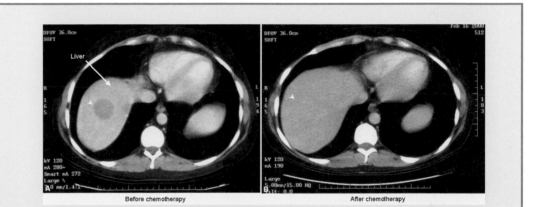

Before chemotherapy                         After chemotherapy

**Figure 6.3** This patient was transplanted with a kidney from a donor with lung cancer. Metastatic lung cancer cells had invaded the kidney before transplantation. In the recipient, the cells metastasized from the kidney to the liver (white arrow). This is the dark circle in the liver on the CT scan (white arrow head). Fortunately for this patient, chemotherapy cured the metastastis to the liver. (*John Wiley & Sons, Inc.*)

months after receiving the new kidney. For these reasons, donor organs are scrutinized very carefully to minimize the chances of transmitting a deadly cargo.

red blood cells that normally travel through these capillaries), so they may simply stick in the capillaries and block the blood flow. Often they attract **platelets** in the blood. These are rich in growth factors, which play an important role in wound healing. These growth factors can help the cancer cell survive and grow in its new location.

To get into the tissue of the new organ, the cancer cell must breach the wall of the capillary, either by invading between the cells or, if it starts to proliferate in the capillary, it may rupture the capillary wall. Each of our tissues has a characteristic extracellular matrix of proteins, and in each tissue the resident cells express particular adhesion receptor proteins that recognize its particular type of extracellular matrix. In order to successfully establish a metastatic colony in a new organ, the cancer cell must make (or begin to make) a suitable adhesion receptor so that it can survive in its new environment. This limitation in tumor cell–body organ compatibility is probably one of the main factors that governs the patterns of metastasis from primary tumors in particular tissues. Some destinations are much more attractive to tumor cells than others, and it is in these destinations that metastatic colonies will be most frequently found.

## SUMMARY

Cells that escape from an invasive cancer can spread to other sites in the body via the blood or lymphatic circulation. The formation of metastatic colonies of cancer cells requires that the cancer cells and the new host tissue are compatible. Metastatic cancer is very difficult to treat because the secondary tumors can be so widespread and difficult to find.

# 7

## CANCER DETECTION AND DIAGNOSIS

**KEY POINTS**

♦ Many countries have established screening programs to detect cancers in the population at early stages.

♦ If something suspicious is found by a screening, a biopsy is performed to obtain a tissue sample for analysis.

♦ Several diagnostic tests are performed by a pathologist on the tissue sample to determine whether it is a tumor and to guide the treatment options for the patient.

Until the middle of the twentieth century, most cancer patients came to the doctor with advanced malignancies that had already spread to other organs. This delay in diagnosis contributed greatly to the low survival time associated with these tumors. Because cancer research and public awareness have improved, tumors of many organs are now being found much sooner than previously, so there is a better chance to detect the cancer before it spreads to other sites. Many different screening techniques have been developed that can be applied to entire populations of people at risk for particular cancers. This approach can be a very cost-effective way of reducing mortality from these diseases.

In many cases, it is the patient who first notices a tumor. There may be a mole on the skin that begins to look abnormal by changing shape or getting bigger or perhaps a lump might be noticed in a breast or testicle. Many people are alive today because they noticed these warning signs and visited their doctor right away. Thanks to a number of educational campaigns, there is more information available to the general public on the warning signs for cancer. For example, women are now much more likely than in previous decades to undertake routine breast self-examinations, which can lead to early identification of potentially harmful growths.

## SCREENING FOR CANCER: MANY BENEFITS BUT NOT PROBLEM-FREE

For some cancers, diagnostic methods are available that can be applied to all members of the healthy population at intervals, which will help detect cancers at sufficiently early stages to allow successful treatment. This population-based approach can be effective for common tumors such as breast, cervical, and prostate cancers.

However, it is important to realize that cancer screening is subject to errors and mistakes. Sometimes people who don't have cancer will be referred for further testing, while occasionally people who really do have cancer will receive a negative test result. In the first situation, people who do not have disease are subjected to unnecessary stress and worry, while in the second situation, those patients are at higher risk of developing more advanced cancer. Failures in screening (either positive or negative) can cause a lot of stress and anger among the affected patients. Thus, it is important to remember that these screening procedures are not 100 percent accurate, and that problems can and do occur. Despite these imperfections, cancer screening has become a cornerstone of public health in many countries and has saved the lives of many people.

## BREAST CANCER: MAMMOGRAPHY

A **mammogram** (Figure 7.1) is a special low-dose X ray photograph of the breast that can reveal tumors. Doctors recommend that women have a mammogram every two years, starting at age 40. For this procedure, the breast is placed on a platform (Figure 7.2) and compressed to spread out the breast tissue in order to get a better photograph. This procedure is not comfortable but is generally not painful; if it is painful, the patient should inform the X ray technician. Usually, each breast is photographed from the top, bottom, and side. If a woman has breast implants, more photographs are sometimes necessary.

A radiologist then examines the mammograms to make sure everything looks normal. If something seems suspicious, the patient can be referred for further examination, either a sonogram (another imaging of the breast) or a biopsy. A biopsy involves the removal of a small tissue sample from the suspicious region to determine if there is a tumor. Approximately 6 to 7 percent of positive mammograms turn out to be false positives, or with no tumors found, much to the relief to the patient and her family. Mammography has reduced death rates from breast cancer by up to 30 percent.

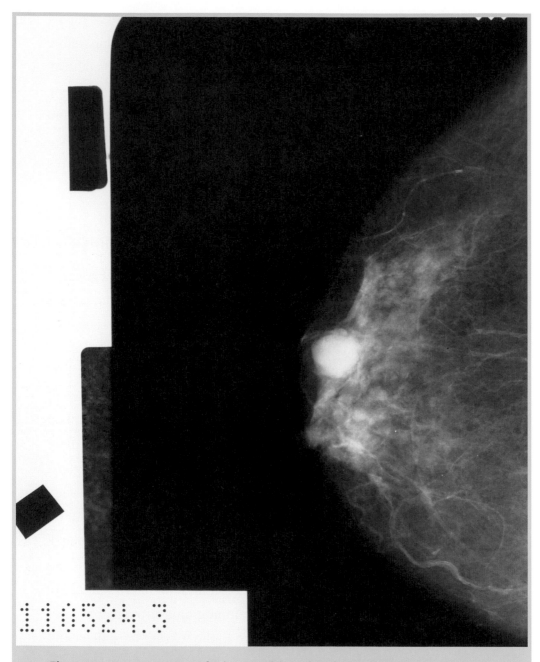

**Figure 7.1** A mammogram of a breast with a whitish area diagnosed as colloid carcinoma. (*National Cancer Institute/U.S. National Institutes of Health*)

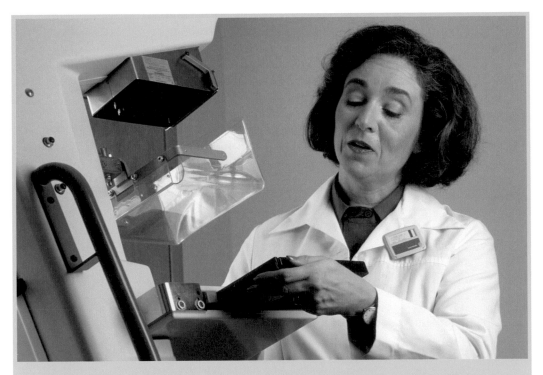

**Figure 7.2** A mammography technician with a mammography machine. (*National Cancer Institute/U.S. National Institutes of Health*)

## PROSTATE CANCER: DRE AND PSA

The prostate gland is a small chestnut-sized gland found in males and located just below the bladder and surrounding the urethra (near the rectum). The prostate secretes some of the fluid in semen. Prostate cancer is common among older men. Fortunately, two different tests are available that can help diagnose this disease at an early stage. PSA (prostate-specific antigen) is a protein secreted by the normal prostate gland and circulates at low levels in the blood. In prostate cancer, however, the levels of PSA in the blood are greatly elevated and can be detected with a special test. The other test, the digital rectal examination (DRE), involves the doctor placing a gloved and lubricated finger inside the rectum and feeling for lumps or abnormal firmness in the prostate gland. While some men find this test uncomfortable and a little embarrassing, they should not forget that this is a

---

### ♦ GEORGE PAPANIKOLAOU AND THE PAP TEST

Cancer of the cervix was once one of the major killers of women in the developed world. It is largely caused by a virus, the human papillomavirus, which is spread by sexual contact. In 1928, George Papanikolaou (1883-1962), a Greek physician working at Cornell Medical School, published the results of his investigations into the microscopic appearance of cells, or **cytology,** of the cervix. The cervix is the neck of the uterus, located at the top of the vagina. The Pap smear (named after Dr. Papanikolaou) takes place during a normal gynecological examination and involves gently removing some of the surface cells of the cervix with a swab and placing them on a microscope slide. Using special dyes, trained cytologists examine the cells to ensure that they are normal. Sometimes abnormal cells will be detected that may indicate precancerous changes. If so, doctors will recommend a more detailed examination and perhaps a biopsy to determine whether cancer is present.

The Pap smear is a straightforward and inexpensive means of screening women for this potentially deadly cancer. Since its introduction, this test has

very common procedure, performed frequently by doctors. Detection of prostate cancer early, using either or both of these tests, increases the probability that treatment will be successful.

## OTHER SCREENING TESTS

Tests are also available for colon cancer, cervical cancer (see "George Papanikolaou and the Pap Test" box) and skin cancer (see

saved the lives of hundreds of thousands of women in the developed world as earlier detection of cancerous changes allows doctors to intervene. In contrast, cervical cancer mortality rates are still very high in many parts of the developing world where resources are not available to screen the female population. Doctors recommend that women have their first Pap test at age 21 or within three years of their first sexual intercourse, whichever comes first.

**Figure 7.3** George Papanikolaou. (*National Library of Medicine/U.S. National Institutes of Health*)

"The ABCDE Rule for Skin Cancer" box). As we learn more about the different genes and proteins that are commonly deregulated in particular tumor types, more tests will be designed. A lot of energy is currently focused on identifying serum markers of disease, which are soluble proteins present in blood at much higher levels in patients carrying a tumor. Like the PSA test for prostate cancer, these tests promise to be a noninvasive, fast, and cheap way of testing for tumors in the whole population.

## AFTER DETECTION, DIAGNOSIS

Once a cancer is discerned by self-examination, a routine visit with the doctor, or by one of the tests described above, the next step is to confirm the diagnosis. The patient is referred to a specialist who deals regularly with tumors of that type. Usually a biopsy may be performed to confirm that a tumor is present. Biopsies for many organ sites are relatively straightforward procedures. For example, a breast biopsy is often performed by pushing a small, hollow needle into the suspicious region to remove a sample of cells. This procedure is called fine needle aspiration and can often be performed without even using a local anesthetic. In this way, a sample of cells can be removed from the area in question and be examined by a pathologist.

A pathologist will look for abnormalities in the sample that might be indicative of cancer. Cancer cells are often larger than their normal counterparts and the nuclei of cancer cells might have a different shape or size. Tumors also often contain a large number of white blood cells. By examining all aspects of the sample, a pathologist can quickly determine whether cancer is present or not. For example, a swelling that looks important on a mammogram can

### ◆ THE ABCDE RULE FOR SKIN CANCER

Basal cell carcinoma of the skin is the most common human tumor, far more common than breast, lung, or prostate cancers. Cases are too numerous to track for national statistics. These tumors can often be easily treated by minor surgery, if detected in time. Skin cancers usually result from mutations sustained by overexposure to the sun. As the amount of ozone in the atmosphere is reduced, there is less of a protective shield from the sun's ultraviolet rays, so skin cancers are becoming more common. Other skin cancers that are more deadly than basal cell carcinoma include squamous cell carcinoma and malignant melanoma. You can help detect skin cancers on your own body by following the "ABCDE Rule" and consulting your doctor if you notice any problems.

#### Signs of Skin Cancer: The ABCDE Rule

**A** for asymmetry: A mole that, when divided in half, doesn't look the same on both sides.

**B** for border: A mole with edges that are blurry or jagged.

**C** for color: Changes in the color of a mole, including darkening, spread of color, loss of color, or the appearance of multiple colors such as blue, red, white, pink, purple, or gray.

**D** for diameter: A mole larger than a ¼ inch in diameter.

**E** for elevation: A mole that is raised above the skin and has an uneven surface.

often turn out to be a harmless fluid-filled cyst. It is vital to do a biopsy to confirm that cancer is present before undergoing surgery and chemotherapy.

Fine needle aspiration is also used for suspected tumors in the thyroid gland, pancreas, lung, and liver; because the lung, liver, and pancreas are difficult to reach without major surgery, fine needle aspiration provides an excellent method to obtain a small tissue sample for analysis.

Endoscopy is another method used to obtain biopsied material. An endoscope is a long fiber-optic cable with a forceps on the end that can be inserted into several internal body cavities such as the gastrointestinal tract, the bladder, or the trachea and bronchus. The doctor can then view the inside of the body on a monitor and use the forceps to remove a small tissue sample from any region that looks suspicious. This procedure is much less invasive than surgery that opens the abdomen and examines the bowel or intestines.

In addition to just examining the cells, the pathologist will often test for the presence or absence of particular proteins to guide treatment options. For example, two proteins important in breast cancer are called estrogen receptor and *HER2*. The pathologist can measure the amount of each protein that is present in each cell. This information is very useful for planning treatments, because drugs that work against tumors with a lot of estrogen receptor do not work well against tumors with a lot of *HER2*; if a tumor has very little estrogen receptor and a lot of *HER2*, it is appropriate for the doctors to choose a drug that works against *HER2*.

## SUMMARY

Effective screening methods are now available for several common cancers. These techniques allow the discovery of tumors at much earlier stages. The sooner a tumor is found, the higher the chance of a cure because there has been less time for the cancer cells to grow, invade, and metastasize. Screening is, however, never 100 percent accurate, and misdiagnosis is possible. Biopsies are always taken to determine whether cancer is present.

# 8

## AFTER A POSITIVE DIAGNOSIS: TREATMENT AND CURE

> **KEY POINTS**
>
> ♦ For solid tumors, particularly smaller ones, surgery is often the best first option.
>
> ♦ Surgery is often followed by chemotherapy or radiation therapy or a combination of the two.
>
> ♦ These treatments try to kill cancer cells that may have escaped from the primary tumor before surgery.

For many tumors, surgery represents the best option at the earliest stages. The surgical team operates on the patient to remove the primary tumor. If the tumor is very large, sometimes chemotherapy is given for some time before surgery to shrink the tumor to a more manageable size. The surgeon carefully removes the tumor and some of the surrounding tissue, called the margins. After removal, the tumor is sent to another doctor, the pathologist, who specializes in examination of tissues.

The pathologist will perform several tests on the tumor, examining it under a microscope to learn more about it and to suggest possible treatment options. One very important task for the pathologist is to check the margins of the tumor to make sure they are composed of normal cells. If some tumor cells are found on the outside of the surgical specimen, the entire tumor was not removed, and the patient must return to surgery so that the remainder can be removed.

In Chapter 6, we learned that tumor cells often spread to nearby lymph nodes. Often during surgery, the surgeon will remove one or more of the nearby lymph nodes to check for metastatic cancer cells. If the lymph nodes contain tumor cells, the cancer has spread beyond the site of origin and this suggests that tumor cells may already have migrated to other tissues. If there are no tumor cells present in the lymph node, the news is more encouraging. Because invasive tumor cells end up so often in the nearest node, if none are found there it suggests that the cancer was removed before it began to spread. In general, the outlook is a lot better for patients with no lymph node metastases. These are referred to as node-negative patients. For node-positive patients, additional therapy such as chemotherapy is likely to be recommended to help eradicate cancer cells at any distant sites.

## TREATMENTS TO KILL ANY REMAINING TUMOR CELLS

After surgery, and depending on the tumor type, additional therapy may be given. These treatments are designed to kill any cells that the tumor might have shed into the tissue surrounding the tumor site, and also to deal with any distant metastatic tumors cells that may or may not be present. The patient's choice of treatment depends on the tumor type and on what the doctors have learned from the surgery. Every attempt is made to kill any remaining tumor cells. Sometimes **radiation therapy** is applied to the site from which the tumor was removed. Chemotherapy and radiation therapy are particularly toxic to rapidly dividing cells, a common characteristic of tumor cells, and help to reduce the chance of any tumor cells surviving, which may form a recurrent tumor months or years later.

For tackling distant metastases, **chemotherapy** is often a good option. These are usually toxic drugs that will circulate throughout the body and kill rapidly dividing cells. Often at the time of surgery, doctors do not know whether or not metastasis has occurred. The safest course of action is to assume that some tumor cells have escaped from the primary tumor to distant sites in the body, even if these cells can't be detected. The patient is then treated to kill these cells, if indeed they exist. Although often necessary, it can be frustrating both for patients and doctors to treat a disease that they cannot see or detect. The only way of knowing whether or not the treatment has worked is to wait several years to see if the cancer recurs. During this time, patients are monitored frequently by their doctors and are often prescribed drugs that try to prevent the cancer from recurring.

Many chemotherapies are targeted at cells that have a high rate of cell division, which frequently characterizes tumor cells. Tumor cells are not the only cells in the body that divide rapidly, and chemotherapy produces side effects on other cells, such as cells of the bone marrow or intestines. For example, one unfortunate effect of chemotherapy is the loss of hair, because hair is produced by a population of cells that continues to divide in a normal, controlled manner throughout your life. As a result, hair-producing cells are affected by chemotherapy as are any other population of normally dividing cells in your body.

## NON-TARGETED THERAPIES

Treatments applied to cancer can be classified as non-targeted and targeted. For decades, the only treatments available were non-targeted and consisted of toxic chemicals, some derived from experiments with chemical weapons. These chemotherapies are usually toxic to both normal and cancer cells and are often associated with moderate to severe side effects. These compounds can be effective at killing tumor cells, but because they also interact with normal cells, they can be very toxic. A dose is chosen that will, hopefully, kill the cancer cells before it kills the patient.

### Radiation Therapy

X rays were discovered by Wilhelm Roentgen (1845–1923) (Figure 8.1) at the end of the nineteenth century. Roentgen was awarded the Nobel Prize for physics in 1901 for this research. Two years later, Pierre and Marie Curie were awarded the Nobel Prize for their research on the spontaneously radioactive element radium. Together, X rays and radium therapy were quickly applied to cancer treatment, and radiation was shown to significantly improve the response of the tumor to therapy. It was also realized quite early that radiation was a double-edged sword because, in addition to curing cancer, it could actually cause cancer. Many early radiologists developed leukemia because of their exposure to radiation during the course of their work. We now realize that radiation exerts its effects by causing DNA mutations in cells. While high doses can effectively kill cancer cells, even relatively low doses can cause mutations in normal cells and cause them to become cancerous.

**Figure 8.1**  Wilhelm Roentgen discovered X rays. (*National Library of Medicine/U.S. National Institutes of Health*)

During the twentieth century, the delivery of radiation therapy for cancer steadily improved. Now concentrated beams of radiation can be focused directly on the tumor site with minimal damage to adjacent tissues. This technique minimizes the potential for harm that could be caused by the induction of mutations that could initiate the development of entirely new cancers. The localized application of radiation afforded by this new technology also increases the dose that can be given safely to a patient.

## Chemotherapy

Studies of persons exposed to chemical warfare during World War I showed that among the symptoms experienced was a dramatic reduction in white blood cell numbers. This information suggested that these wartime compounds might be useful against cancer cells that, like white blood cells, divide very rapidly. Experiments with one class of these compounds, called nitrogen mustard, showed that they were effective against lymphoma. A drug developed from nitrogen mustard called cyclophosphamide is still in use today. These drugs work by binding to and damaging DNA. Usually, the cell's DNA damage surveillance mechanisms will detect this damage and trigger that cell's self-destruction. These experiments laid the foundation for the chemotherapeutic approach to cancer.

Later drugs were developed that targeted the process of DNA synthesis. Because cancer cells tend to divide much more rapidly than most other cells in the body, suppressing DNA synthesis represented a reasonable way to attack the cancer cell. Sydney Farber (1903–1973) used a compound called aminopterin, which inhibits this process, to successfully treat leukemia in children. Methotrexate, a drug based on aminopterin, is still used in chemotherapy today. In 1956, more than 2,000 years after the first crude investigations of cancer began, the

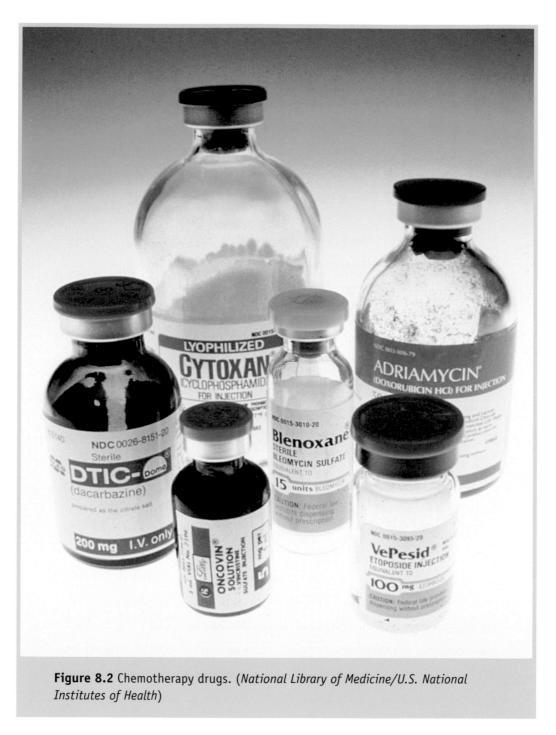

**Figure 8.2** Chemotherapy drugs. (*National Library of Medicine/U.S. National Institutes of Health*)

first cure of a metastatic cancer was reported—the drug involved was methotrexate. Another drug that targets the process of DNA synthesis is 5-fluoro-Uracil (5FU). This compound has a structure very similar to the pyrimidine bases (C and T) that make up DNA, and this similarity allows it to interfere with DNA synthesis. Capecitabine and gemcitabine are two forms of 5FU that are commonly used in chemotherapy today.

Other DNA-damaging drugs that are effective against tumors are two salts of platinum, cisplatin and carboplatin. These chemicals cause bonds to form between the G bases of DNA, thus affecting the cell's ability to duplicate its DNA during cell division. Although this compound was discovered by Michel Peyrone (1813–1865) in 1845, its potential uses as an anticancer agent were not realized until the 1960s, when Barnett Rosenberg (1926) and colleagues at Michigan State University showed that it had the ability to block cell division in *E. coli* bacteria.

After a cell duplicates its DNA, each set of chromosomes moves to opposite ends of the cell on molecular cables made of a protein called tubulin. Interrupting the function of tubulin affects the ability of cancer cells to divide. Two compounds from plants are very effective inhibitors of tubulin. A drug called *taxol* was isolated from the yew tree and a drug called *vincristine* was isolated from another plant, the Madagascar periwinkle. Several derivatives of these drugs are now in clinical use against cancer.

## TARGETED THERAPIES

The second class of treatments, targeted therapies, began to be developed as new molecular insights into the workings of the tumor cell were gained. Many of the signaling proteins that play roles in cancer are **enzymes**—including kinases, proteases and GTPases. Targeted therapies are aimed at developing specific inhibitors for some of these enzymes. A perfect targeted therapy would inhibit an enzyme that is present at high levels in tumor cells and low levels (or not expressed) in normal cells. In this way, the treatment is much more selective than the older chemotherapies using nontargeted drugs.

Two important discoveries suggested that hormonal treatments might be useful for cancers of the breast and prostate. Near the end of the nineteenth century, a Scottish doctor, Thomas Beatson (1848-1933), observed that removal of the ovaries of rabbits prevented milk production in their mammary glands. This observation suggested that a potentially important link might exist between the ovaries and the breasts. He tested this idea by removing the ovaries from women with advanced breast cancer. Excitingly, this treatment led to an improvement in the symptoms of many of these patients. This result suggested that one or more substances produced by the ovaries was causing cancer in the breast to grow. We now know that the primary substance that causes breast tumor growth is the female hormone estrogen.

Unlike many animals, dogs develop prostate cancer relatively frequently. Charles Huggins (1901–1997) (Figure 8.3), a professor of surgery at the University of Chicago, found that removal of the testes (castration) could stop the growth and spread of already established prostate cancers. Like the work of Beatson, Huggins' data indicated that the testes produce some hormones that travel to the prostate and cause the cancer cells to grow. This important discovery paved the way for the use of anti-androgen treatment for prostate cancer. In 1966, Huggins won the Nobel Prize for making this research breakthrough. The prize was shared with Peyton Rous, mentioned in Chapter 2, for his work on Rous sarcoma virus.

**Figure 8.3** Charles Huggins' experiments paved the way for the use of anti-androgen treatment for prostate cancer. (*National Library of Medicine/U.S. National Institutes of Health*)

To avoid the need to surgically remove testes and ovaries, it was necessary to develop drugs that blocked the effect of their hormones. One of the earliest targeted drug therapies was tamoxifen. This drug is a molecule with a very similar shape to estrogen, and targets and binds to a receptor within the cell for estrogen, an important hormone for female development. More than half of all human breast cancers are enriched in this receptor. Unlike estrogen, which switches on the receptor when it binds, tamoxifen inactivates the receptor. Many women with this type of breast cancer are now breast cancer survivors thanks to this life-saving drug.

As more and more genes and proteins are identified as important in cancer development and progression, scientists are busily trying to develop ways to inhibit them. Some of these targeted therapies are

---

### ◆ SIDE EFFECTS OF CHEMOTHERAPY

Many chemotherapies can be essentially thought of as poisons that kill rapidly dividing cells. While most cells in an adult divide relatively slowly (if at all), cells in a number of tissues proliferate more quickly. Common side effects of chemotherapy occur in tissues with high rates of cell division such as hair follicles, bone marrow, and intestines, leading to hair loss, nausea and vomiting, diarrhea, and anemia. Because white blood cell proliferation is suppressed in chemotherapy, the body's immune system may be greatly weakened. In some cases a bone marrow transplant is used to restore the crucial **stem cells** killed by the treatment. After division, stem cells replace their own numbers

already on the market and used by patients. Herceptin is an antibody targeting cells that overexpress a cell-surface signaling protein called *HER2*. *HER2* is found at high levels in approximately one-third of breast cancers, and this drug has been shown to kill tumor cells in these breast cancer patients.

Sometimes despite the best efforts of the doctors and the patient, the cancer returns. It may come back either at the original site or at a distant site. At this point, the doctors and patient must consult and decide what to do. If it seems that the new tumor mass is localized, surgery to remove it may be an appropriate treatment. In other cases, such as when metastatic tumor growth is found at many sites, more chemotherapy might be used to try to bring the disease under control.

and also give rise to cells that differentiate further into one or more specialized types.

As chemotherapy has become more advanced, doctors have developed strategies to combat some of its side effects. For example, antiemetic drugs (to prevent vomiting) are now administered with chemotherapy to reduce the amount of nausea experienced by the patient. There have been several reports that marijuana (either smoked or consumed as a tea) can greatly diminish the side effects experienced by patients during chemotherapy.

Cancer researchers hope to identify less toxic and more specific methods of targeting cancer cells. These treatments should more effectively target the tumor, with minimal side effects for the rest of the body.

## SUMMARY

After a surgeon has removed the primary tumor, doctors usually prescribe chemotherapy and/or radiation therapy to help eradicate any remaining cancer cells in the body. These are relatively crude treatments that can harm normal as well as cancer cells. Several drugs have been developed that are more effective at specifically targeting cancer cells. These medications offer hope for less toxic and more effective treatments of cancer.

# 9

# IF TREATMENT FAILS

**KEY POINTS**

♦ Even years after the initial surgery and treatment, cancer may return.

♦ Cancers can recur when some of the original tumor cells remain in the body.

♦ New cancer drugs are subjected to rigorous testing in human participants in a series of clinical trials. These trials are regulated by the U.S. Food and Drug Administration.

Cancers thought to have been cured can sometimes return months or even years after surgery. This event is known as **recurrence**, and can happen because not all of the original cancer cells were eradicated by the initial treatment. Recurrences are classified as local, regional, or distant. Local recurrence is the reappearance of a tumor at or near the site of the original cancer. Regional recurrence is the reappearance of tumor cells in the lymph nodes or other tissues near the location of the removal of the original tumor. In the case of distant recurrence, the growth comes from cancer cells that had escaped from the primary tumor before surgery and metastasized to another part of the body.

It is important to realize that the recurrence is not a new cancer, even if many years have passed since the patient was first treated. The tumors develop from cells originating from the primary cancer, which can lie dormant in the body for long periods of time. Tumor recurrence is understandably very difficult for patients, who up until that point were relieved to believe themselves to be cancer-free.

As with primary tumors, the treatment options for recurrent cancer include surgery, radiotherapy, and chemotherapy. The choice depends on many factors, such as the size of the recurrent tumor and whether it is localized to a particular point in the body or is more widely dispersed. The general health of the patient is also considered, as is the probability of success of the treatment. Depending on the tumor type and the extent of the recurrence, the treatment may be aimed at curing the cancer or at shrinking it and keeping it in check to extend the life of the patient.

Unfortunately, in many cases of recurrent metastatic cancer, the long-term prospects of survival may be low. If this is the case, it is important that the patient, in conjunction with the medical team, makes informed decisions to ensure the best possible quality of life. In some cases, treatment may extend the life of the patient for many years, while in other cases even very aggressive treatment may provide little benefit in terms of increased survival time.

## WHEN THERE IS NO HOPE FOR CURE

The time comes for many cancer patients, after the recurrence of a primary tumor and after metastasis, to face the fact that the cancer has spread throughout the body beyond the reach of the surgeon's knife. By this time, the cancer patient will often have been through surgery, radiation therapy, and several cycles of different chemotherapeutic drugs as each new recurrence was detected. The cancer cells in the body have survived so many attempts to kill them that they are now resistant to chemotherapy. As well as being a very sad time for the patient and family, it is also a sobering reminder to those in the medical and cancer research community that, despite all of the best efforts over many decades, we are still losing patients to this pernicious and resilient disease and that much more work remains to be done.

There are several excellent publications and Web sites devoted to discussing the many problems and emotions that cancer patients and their families face as they approach the end of life, and a detailed discussion of these issues is beyond the scope of this book. A number of these resources are listed in the Further Reading section. Nevertheless, because death still often comes after a long battle with cancer, we will briefly look at some of these issues here.

When it becomes apparent that the cancer is so widely dispersed in the body and that all of the standard treatments have been used, the chances of that patient becoming cured are remote. At this stage, the medical care received by the patient is often aimed at **palliation**, the easing of the symptoms of the disease without aiming to cure the disease itself.

Hospice care (Figure 9.1) helps to provide comfort and support to a person in the final stages of cancer, with the emphasis on improving the quality of the remainder of that person's life rather than on aggressive treatment of the cancer. Emotional and psychological support play important parts in hospice care. Hospice care treats the whole person, rather than just the cancer cells. Drugs are used, often morphine, to

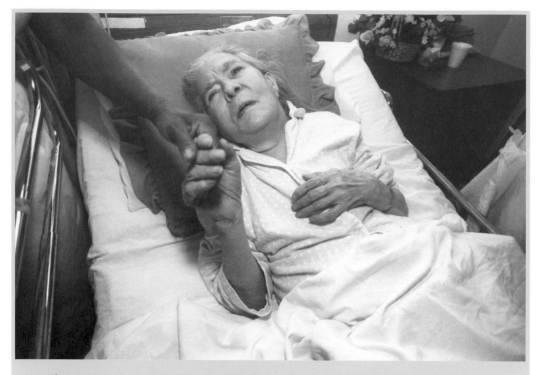

**Figure 9.1** A sympathetic nurse holds an elderly woman's hand in hospice. (*Abraham Menashe/Photo Researchers, Inc.*)

control the pain that may occur in the later stages of the disease. Hospice care can be provided in the patient's home, nursing home, or hospital. The hospice movement was begun by Cicely Saunders (1918–2005) in England in 1967, and the first hospice in the United States was opened by Florence Wald (1917– ) in 1974. There are now more than 3,000 hospice care programs across the country.

When established medical treatments have failed to control the cancer, there are still options available for patients determined to continue an aggressive battle against their cancer. As new drugs are constantly in development, there are opportunities to participate in clinical trials and obtain access to these drugs in the earliest phases of testing. Volunteers are offered the possibility of being among the first to benefit if the drug on the trial turns out to have a positive effect in that particular tumor type.

Unfortunately, in their desperation to find a cure, many patients try dubious and untested therapies, often promoted over the Internet. These can be expensive therapies that deprive the cancer patient and their family of large sums of money without providing any effective benefit (see "Taking Advantage of Cancer Patients" sidebar). Furthermore, some of these treatments may encourage the patient to stop taking a prescribed medication that may actually help to keep the cancer in check.

## CLINICAL TRIALS

Before they are released to the general patient population, all drugs are subjected to a series of stringent tests called clinical trials. These trials are regulated by the U.S. Food and Drug Administration (FDA). A drug cannot be prescribed by a doctor until it has been approved for specific conditions or uses by the FDA. There are many new drugs in development for cancer treatment at various stages of the clinical trials process. There are three main stages of a clinical trial in human volunteers—Phase I, Phase II, and Phase III trials—with drugs only entering human clinical trials after several studies in mice and other animals.

Phase I studies are the first step of the testing process in humans and aim to provide information about how well the drug is tolerated by patients. Because it is an experimental treatment about which so little is known, Phase I cancer drug studies usually involve a relatively small

---

### ♦ TAKING ADVANTAGE OF CANCER PATIENTS

Many cancer patients, desperate to survive and willing to try anything, fall victim to frauds offering dubious treatments, often over the Internet, which claim to cure cancer. To take advantage of terminally ill cancer patients is reprehensible. In one famous case, Harry Hoxsey ran a clinic in Dallas, Texas, from 1936 until he was eventually shut down by the United States Food and Drug Administration (FDA) in 1960. He claimed to treat terminally ill cancer patients using a tonic derived from various roots and tree barks. It has been estimated that he earned $50 million from selling this tonic to many thousands of desperate people.

The market for these cures in the United States has been estimated at $4 billion annually. Tijuana, Mexico, is the home of the greatest concentration of "hospitals" and "clinics" which provide these "cures" to patients today. Because these clinics operate outside of FDA jurisdiction, there are no restrictions on what they can legally claim. Vulnerable patients and their families may spend vast sums of money—up to $40,000 per treatment—for these questionable treatments. However, the Mexican government has been cracking down on some of these clinics in recent years.

---

number of patients with advanced metastatic cancer whose tumors no longer respond to standard therapies. In Phase I studies, doctors try to work out the best way to administer the drug to patients, for example, by mouth or by intravenous drip. The patients are usually divided into small groups, each receiving a different dose of the drug. This type of study allows the doctors to determine how much of the drug can be tolerated by humans and what side effects are observed. After performing a Phase I clinical trial, doctors have a good idea what the best dose of the drug is likely to be.

If a drug is well tolerated, the next step is to begin a Phase II study using the dosing guidelines obtained from Phase I. Phase II studies are aimed at determining whether the drug is effective against tumors. Because the treatment is still experimental and because it may be no better than (or not as good as) the prevailing standard treatment, Phase II studies typically recruit a relatively small number of participants. The patients and their tumors are closely monitored for the duration of the trial to see if the treatment has any effect on the tumor. Depending on the tumor type, results can be assessed in a number of ways. Skin tumors may be measured directly. Tumors in internal organs such as the liver or lungs can be examined using X rays or computerized tomography (CT) scans. To be successful in a Phase II study, a drug needs to at least reduce the size or stop the growth of the tumor in a number of the participants. Such a result shows that the drug is potentially effective against this type of cancer.

The next step in the drug-testing process, Phase III, is to determine how the drug compares to the current standard treatment for that disease. By this point, doctors already know a lot about which doses have been effective against tumors and what doses they can safely dispense to patients. Unlike Phase I and II studies, Phase III clinical trials usually recruit a large number of patients. Depending on the trial, there are often limitations on what type of patient can be enrolled to ensure that the population of patients in the trial is well-balanced with respect to age, gender, tumor type and stage, and previous treatment history. Having a balanced patient population in the trial helps to prevent any potential bias and to ensure that any effects that are seen are due to the drug and not to a difference in the treatment groups. For this reason, patients are usually divided into treatment groups in a process called randomization. In one straightforward type of Phase III trial, two treatment groups receive the

---

### ◆ A PROMISING TARGETED THERAPY

Figure 9.2A is from a 54-year-old woman with a metastatic gastro-intestinal stromal tumor, a tumor for which there is usually little chance of a cure. When she was diagnosed at age 50, two tumor masses (6.5 and 10 centimeters in diameter) were removed from her stomach. Two years later, the cancer recurred and two liver metastases and several abdominal metastases were surgically removed. Seven months later, six further metastases were removed from her liver and a metastasis was removed from an ovary. She was then given six treatments of multiple chemotherapies to treat many more liver metastases. Four months after her previous operation, she underwent surgery again to remove a large metastatic tumor from her bowel and 45 other smaller metastases. In less than a year, several more metastases were detected in the liver and throughout the abdomen. From what you have learned in reading this book, you know that this patient clearly did not have a good prognosis. In the scan on the left, each of the black patches represents metastatic tumor colonies.

This patient took part in the study of an experimental treatment for her type of tumor. The drug, Gleevec, is a specific inhibitor of the enzyme that causes a gastrointestinal stromal tumor. Figure 9.2B is a scan taken of the patient after only four weeks of treatment with the new drug. The amount of tumor has been very substantially reduced. (The lowest black

standard treatment (e.g., chemotherapy), and one group also receives the experimental treatment while the second group receives a sugar pill, called the placebo (Figure 9.3). Patients are not told which group they

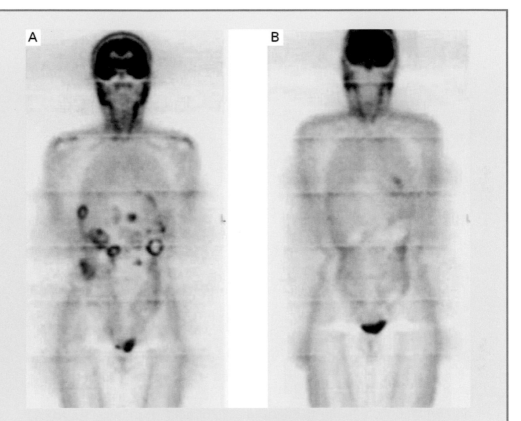

**Figure 9.2** Effect of the tyrosine kinase inhibitor ST1571 (Gleevec) in a patient with a metastatic gastrointestinal stromal tumor. The scan on the left was before treatment and the scan on the right is after four weeks of treatment with Gleevec. (© 2001 Massachusetts Medical Society. All rights reserved. )

patch in both images is not a tumor—it is the bladder, where the labeling dye used to take the image accumulates.)

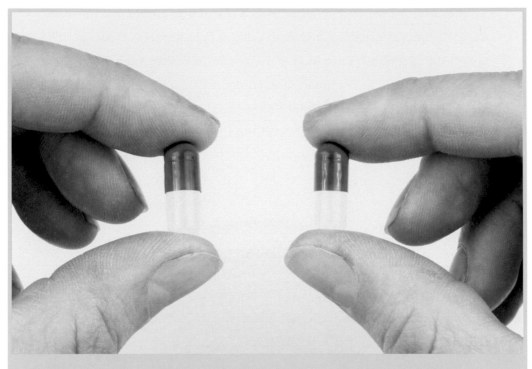

**Figure 9.3** Hands holding two identical capsules, one of which is medically inactive (a placebo), while the other is a drug or medicine. (*Cordelia Molloy/ Photo Researchers, Inc.*)

are in. A trial like this will show if the experimental drug provides any additional benefit to the standard treatment, such as increased survival rates or a more pronounced effect on tumor shrinkage.

## WHY PARTICIPATE IN CLINICAL TRIALS?

Patient participation in clinical trials is entirely voluntary. Why do they do it? Many patients express a sincere desire to help in the development of newer, better treatments so that future cancer patients will have more effective treatments. This attitude is particularly common  among patients in Phase I clinical trials, who are usually terminally ill with no hope of a cure from existing treatments. Often the possibility that the new treatment may help to treat their cancer is a strong motivating factor. In general, if a new treatment is successful, the patients in the clinical trial are the first to benefit, and being enrolled in a clinical trial is the only route by which patients can obtain the latest cancer treatments. Of course, it must be remembered that the efficacy of these treatments is unproven until the end of the Phase III study and that the newer treatment might prove to be less effective than the standard treatment for that cancer, and may have unforeseen side effects.

## SUMMARY

When a cancer recurs, there are often a number of treatment options still available, which can cure the cancer or at least keep it in remission for many years. If the cancer becomes widespread and resistant to treatment, the death of the patient may be the outcome. New targeted drugs offer tremendous hope for the future of cancer therapy. As researchers develop more treatments, it will become possible to more effectively control and cure cancer.

# 10

## FUTURE PERSPECTIVES

---

**KEY POINTS**

♦ In the past 40 years, there has been remarkable progress in our understanding of human cancer.

♦ We are on the verge of a new era of cancer medicine in which specially targeted drugs will be given to patients depending on the molecular characteristics of their tumors.

---

As we have seen in earlier chapters, our recognition of cancer in humans stretches back several thousand years, but it is only in the last few centuries—and in particular the past few decades—that major breakthroughs have been made in understanding the fundamental biology that underlies this complex group of more than 200 diseases. Although cancer is still a feared disease, the mortality statistics are better now than at any point in history. Thanks to rapid advances in our understanding of the molecular biology and genetics of cancer in the last 40 years, a large array of treatments are now in development that offer the hope of target-ing the specific vulnerabilities of the tumor cell. We have achieved some spectacular successes—for example, 95 percent of testicular cancers can now be cured—but some cancers, such as those of the pancreas and lung, are very resistant to current therapies. More work needs to be done to identify the Achilles' heel of these tumor types.

Many researchers believe that we are rapidly approaching an era of individualized cancer therapy. We now have the technology to take a tumor sample from a patient and measure the expression level of each of the genes in the human genome in that sample. As we better under-stand the role of these genes and the interactions between them in the cancer phenotype, personalized treatment for each patient, dependent on the particular abnormalities in their tumor, becomes a distinct pos-sibility. Up until now, cancers in many tissues have been treated as a single group. It has not been well understood why some tumors from a given tissue respond well to treatment while other tumors from the same tissue continue to grow and kill the patient. Now we will have the power to predict, at the time of surgery, which tumors are likely to recur. This ability to make more accurate prognoses is important to avoid the current overtreatment of patients with chemotherapy. Because we lack good ways to predict which tumors are likely to recur after surgery, all patients are routinely given radiation therapy and/or chemotherapy. Among these patients is a group for whom the chances of recurrence are very remote, but because we can't identify them by current methods, they experience the trauma of chemotherapy unnecessarily.

A test based on gene expression has now been developed that predicts the probability that breast tumors will recur after surgery. If trials with this test are successful, this approach will be applied to other tumor types. These tests would allow us to focus medical attention and treatment on those patients most likely to benefit and to spare those patients whose tumors are unlikely to return from long courses of chemotherapy.

## THE IMPORTANCE OF BASIC RESEARCH

In 1971 President Richard Nixon (1913–1994) signed the National Cancer Act, which started the "war on cancer." As a result, there was a large increase in the amount of money available for cancer research (Table 10.1), which led to dramatic improvements in our understanding of many areas of basic mammalian biology and of the inner workings of the cancer cell. In recent years, this tremendous investment of money and scientific effort has begun to pay off in terms of newer, more effective targeted therapies for patients. I expect that within the next decade, the number of these treatments will increase several-fold.

The war on cancer has been criticized in some quarters for its failure to deliver cures. A comparison has been made to the U.S. space program, which put men on the moon in 1969. Although this "giant leap for mankind" was undoubtedly one of the great achievements of humanity, it was essentially a question of developing rockets of sufficient power to escape the Earth's gravitational pull. It was a technological leap forward rather than a purely scientific one. From a scientific perspective, the mathematics and physics necessary to put a man on the moon were developed by Isaac Newton (1642–1727) 300 years ago. What was primarily needed was an advance in technology and engineering, not in science.

In stark contrast, when the war on cancer began, we had very little scientific knowledge about the structure, genetics, and biology of normal and cancer cells. It has taken a monumental amount of effort by tens of thousands of individuals to crack the secrets of these cells and to begin to understand how they work and interact with each other.

Intensive research by many dedicated scientists has brought us to where we are today and much more research needs to be done before cancer can be comfortably relegated to the status of a treatable and controllable condition. Cancer research has historically been the preserve of clinicians and biologists. In the past 10 years, however, we have recognized that the complex biology of this disease requires additional expertise from people not traditionally involved in cancer research. There has been an explosive growth of multidisciplinary teams to investigate the unexplored frontiers of cancer cell biology. Physicists, mathematicians, computer scientists,

| TABLE 10.1   INCREASES IN THE NATIONAL CANCER INSTITUTE BUDGET | |
|---|---|
| YEAR | NATIONAL CANCER INSTITUTE BUDGET |
| 1946 | $549,000 |
| 1947 | $1.8 million |
| 1961 | $111 million |
| 1973 | $492 million |
| 1980 | $1 billion |
| 1996 | $2.25 billion |
| 2000 | $3.30 billion |
| 2005 | $4.80 billion |
| Source: http://www.nih.gov/about/almanac/appropriations/index.htm | |

and chemists now play very important roles in many laboratories and the skills they bring to the table are proving invaluable in furthering research. For example, physicists play important roles in the study of

---

### ◆ PINKWASHING

---

Many charities exist to raise awareness of and funds for cancer patients and for research into the causes of cancer. The funds raised by these organizations make a very valuable contribution. Some marketing strategies employed by corporate donors, particularly in the area of breast cancer research, are more self-aggrandizing. October is National Breast Cancer Awareness month in the United States, and each year consumers are faced with a bewildering array of pink ribbons, pink lipstick, pink yogurt containers, pink T-shirts, and even pink M&M candies to raise money for breast cancer. While some of these efforts may be genuinely worthwhile, it seems that many of them exist to sell more products, to greatly increase corporate profit, and to boost the image of corporations by associating them with the good cause of breast cancer research.

Many people support these campaigns out of the genuine belief that they are doing something positive to help breast cancer, but it pays to take a cold, hard look at what each company is offering before parting with your money. For example, American Express recently ran a campaign in which they offered to donate one cent to breast cancer research with each transaction. This campaign was designed to encourage people to use their American Express card more often while improving the reputation of

radiation-induced cancers and computer scientists and mathematicians help to build complex mathematical models of biological processes such as signal transduction.

American Express. However, you would need to use your American Express card 1,000 times in order to contribute just $10 to breast cancer research.

Another example is Yoplait yogurt's promise to contribute 10 cents to breast cancer research for each yogurt container lid mailed in (it is not enough to buy the yogurt, you actually have to wash and mail the lid to the company). Ten cents per container seems a greater contribution than American Express's one cent per transaction, but you would have to eat three containers of yogurt a day for one month to raise $10 for breast cancer. Each year, no matter how many lids are mailed, Yoplait donates a maximum of $1.5 million to breast cancer research from this campaign. Yoplait's parent company, General Mills, says in its *Corporate Social Responsibility Report*: "Many General Mills brands have become almost synonymous with important causes close to the hearts of people everywhere." Sales of Yoplait are more than $1 billion a year according to the company's annual report.

If you really want to make a contribution to cancer research, it would be better to write a check for $10 and mail it to the charity of your choice. That will leave you feeling a lot better than if you had just swallowed 100 containers of yogurt! For more information on the issue of marketing in breast cancer fund-raising, visit the Breast Cancer Action Web site: http://www.thinkbeforeyoupink.org/.

One of the landmark advances in human biology in the past decade was the sequencing of the human genome. Finally, we have within our grasp the identity and location of all the genes that make up the body. Of course, the task remains to decipher what many of these genes actually do. Still, in order to understand how any system works, it is extremely useful to have a list of the component parts. In many cases, we can get clues to the function of a gene by looking at its sequence, because it may be related (that is, have a similar sequence) to genes that we have already characterized.

Another aspect of gene regulation that is proving to be important in cancer research is the area of epigenomics, or mechanisms of gene regulation that result from the modification of DNA. During human development, the expression of one copy of a gene is often switched off by a process called **methylation**. The first part of the gene sequence gets chemically modified by enzymes in the cell in such a way that it prevents the gene from being expressed. Methylation is an important way to regulate some growth-specific genes during embryonic development. In cancer, however, this developmental process is often hijacked. We learned about tumor suppressor genes, which help to restrain cell proliferation, in Chapter 4. Sometimes the function of these genes is lost by mutation. We are now realizing that the expression of these genes can also be switched off by methylation. Turning off tumor suppressor gene expression, it provides cancer cells with a big growth advantage by removing one of the critical controls over cell proliferation. Researchers now perform large-scale surveys of the genomes of cancer cells to identify which genes have been switched off by this methylation process, and drugs have been developed to reverse the methylation and potentially switch these vital genes back on.

## WILL THERE EVER BE A CURE FOR CANCER?

In the early days of the war on cancer, it was often hoped that one day they would find a cure for cancer—a "magic bullet" that would seek out and destroy cancer cells throughout the body. Over the past 40 years, we have learned a tremendous amount about the diversity of these 200 diseases that we call cancer. Although there is much overlap in the biology of these diseases, the number of differences between them make it unlikely that a single cure will ever be found. Instead, scientists have focused on identifying the molecular abnormalities peculiar to each cancer and developing treatments to target these abnormalities. So, although we may never find that so-called magic bullet, we will soon have an array of mini-bullets that we can mix-and-match depending on the characteristics of the individual tumor. It is hoped that these cocktails will prove much more effective than the "cut it out, burn it out, and poison it" approach of surgery, radiation therapy, and chemotherapy.

## SUMMARY

We have made much progress in our understanding of cancer and while there may not be a single cure for this disease, the combination of several new drugs should be sufficient to treat the majority of cancers in the not-too-distant future. These advances have been the product of the contributions of thousands of individuals working in laboratories on different aspects of the cancer problem, and of those great doctors, clinicians, and epidemiologists of the past 2,500 years who put us on the right track toward making these discoveries.

# GLOSSARY

◆

**angiogenesis**   Blood vessel formation. Tumor angiogenesis is the growth of blood vessels from surrounding tissue to a solid tumor. Angiogenesis is caused by the release of signaling proteins by the tumor.

**basement membrane**   A thin, delicate layer of connective tissue underlying the epithelium of many organs.

**bases**   The building blocks of DNA and RNA—adenine (A), cytosine (C), guanine (G), and thymine (T), and, in RNA only, uracil. Also called nucleotides.

**benign**   Not cancerous. Benign tumors do not spread to tissues around them or to other parts of the body.

**biopsy**   The removal of cells or tissues for examination by a pathologist. When only a sample of tissue is removed, the procedure is called an incisional biopsy. When an entire lump or suspicious area is removed, the procedure is called an excisional biopsy. When a sample of tissue or fluid is removed with a needle, the procedure is called a needle biopsy, core biopsy, or fine needle aspiration.

**carcinoma in situ**   An early cancer that has not spread to nearby tissues.

**cell cycle**   The series of events involving the growth, replication, and division of a eukaryotic cell.

**cell division**   The process of splitting of somatic cells in which each daughter cell receives the same amount of DNA as the parent cell.

**chemotherapy**   Treatment with drugs that kill cancer cells.

**chromosome**   Part of a cell nucleus that contains genetic information. Except for sperm and eggs, all human cells contain 46 chromosomes.

**cytology**   The study of the microscopic appearance of cells, especially for the diagnosis of abnormalities and malignancies.

**differentiation**   In cancer, description of how mature (developed) the cancer cells are in a tumor. Differentiated tumor cells resemble normal cells and tend to grow and spread at a slower rate than un-differentiated or poorly differentiated tumor cells, which lack the structure and function of normal cells and grow uncontrollably.

**DNA**   Deoxyribonucleic acid. The molecules inside cells that carry genetic information and pass it from one generation to the next.

**dysplasia**   Cells that look abnormal under a microscope but are not yet cancer.

**endothelial cell**   The main type of cell found in the inside lining of blood vessels, lymph vessels, and the heart.

**enzyme**   A protein that speeds up chemical reactions in the body.

**epithelium**   A thin layer of tissue that covers organs, glands, and other structures within the body.

**familial (familial cancer)**   Cancer that occurs in families more often than would be expected by chance; hereditary cancer. These cancers often occur at an early age and may indicate the presence of a gene mutation that increases the risk of cancer. They may also be a sign of shared environmental or lifestyle factors.

**hematopoietic stem cells**   Blood-forming stem cells in the bone marrow.

**hyperplasia**   An abnormal increase in the number of cells in an organ or tissue.

**hypoxia**   A condition in which there is a decrease in the oxygen supply to a tissue. In cancer treatment, the level of hypoxia in a tumor may help predict the response of the tumor to the treatment.

**invasive cancer**   Cancer that has spread beyond the layer of tissue in which it developed and is growing into surrounding, healthy tissues.

**kinase**   An enzyme that catalyzes the addition of a phosphate group ($PO_4^{2-}$) to another molecule.

**lymph node**   A rounded mass of lymphatic tissue that is surrounded by a capsule of connective tissue. Lymph nodes filter lymph (lymphatic fluid) and they store lymphocytes (white blood cells). They are located along lymphatic vessels. Also called a lymph gland.

**lymphatic system**   The lymphatic system is a complex network of lymphoid organs, lymph nodes, lymph ducts, lymph tissues, lymph capillaries, and lymph vessels that produce and transport lymph fluid from tissues to the circulatory system. The lymphatic system is a major component of the immune system.

**malignant**   Cancerous. Malignant tumors can invade and destroy nearby tissue and spread to other parts of the body.

**mammogram**   An X ray of the breast.

**metastasis**   The spread of a cancer tumor from one part of the body to another. The metastatic tumor contains cells that are like those in the original (primary) tumor.

**methylation**   The addition of a methyl ($CH_3$) group to another molecule. Methylation of a region of DNA generally switches off the genes in that region.

**mutation**   Any change in the DNA of a cell. Mutations may be caused by mistakes during cell division or by exposure to DNA-damaging agents in the environment. Mutations can be harmful, beneficial, or have no effect. If they occur in cells that make eggs or sperm, mutations can be inherited; if mutations occur in other types of cells, they are not inherited from one generation to the next. Certain mutations may lead to cancer or other diseases.

**oncogene**   A gene that normally directs cell growth. If altered, an oncogene can promote or allow the uncontrolled growth of cancer. Alterations can be inherited or caused by an environmental exposure to carcinogens.

**palliation**   Care given to improve the quality of life of patients who have a serious or life-threatening disease. The goal of palliative care is to prevent or treat as early as possible the symptoms of the disease, side effects caused by treatment of the disease, and psychological, social, and spiritual issues related to the disease or its treatment. Also called comfort care, supportive care, and symptom management.

**phenotype**   The expression of a specific trait, such as stature or blood type, based on genetic and environmental influences.

**platelet**   A minute, irregularly shaped, disk-like cytoplasmic body found in blood plasma that promotes blood clotting and has no definite nucleus, no DNA, and no hemoglobin.

**protease**   An enzyme that catalyzes the breakdown of other proteins.

**protein**   A molecule made of amino acids that is needed for the body to function properly. Proteins are the basis of body structures, such as skin and hair, and of substances such as enzymes, cytokines, and antibodies.

**proto-oncogene**   Normal copies in the cell, mainly functioning to regulate the rate of cell division. If proto-oncogenes are mutated in body cells, for example, by smoking, radiation, or a random mistake during cell division—cancer may result.

**radiation therapy**   The use of high-energy radiation from X rays, gamma rays, neutrons, and other sources to kill cancer cells and shrink tumors. Radiation may come from a machine outside the body (external-beam radiation therapy) or from radioactive material placed in the body near cancer cells (internal radiation therapy, implant radiation, or brachytherapy). Systemic radiation therapy uses a radioactive substance, such as a radio-labeled monoclonal antibody, that circulates throughout the body.

**recurrence**   Cancer that has returned after a period of time during which the cancer could not be detected. The cancer may come back to the same place as the original (primary) tumor or to another place in the body.

**RNA**   Ribonucleic acid. One of the two types of nucleic acids found in all cells; the other is deoxyribonucleic acid or DNA. RNA translates genetic information from DNA to proteins produced by the cell. Like DNA, RNA contains four bases however the Thymidine (T) base found in DNA is replaced by Uracil (U).

**signal transduction**   The process by which signals are transmitted from the outside of the cell via carrier proteins to the nucleus and other internal structures.

**signaling proteins**   Proteins that initiate or carry signals between cells and from the outside of a cell to internal compartments.

**sporadically (sporadic cancer)**   Cancer that occurs at random in the population. Sporadic cancer contrasts with familial (hereditary) cancer, in which the predisposition to develop the disease is inherited from one or both parents.

**stage**   The extent of a cancer in the body. Staging is usually based on the size of the tumor, whether lymph nodes contain cancer, and if the cancer has spread from the original site to other parts of the body.

**stem cell**   A cell that upon division replaces its own numbers and also gives rise to cells that differentiate further into one or more specialized types.

**stroma**   The connective tissue framework of an organ, gland, or other structure, as distinguished from the tissues performing the special function of the organ or part.

**tumor suppressor gene**   A type of gene (unit of heredity passed from parent to offspring) that helps inhibit cell growth. Blocking the action of tumor suppressor genes may lead to cancer.

**vasculature**   The arrangement of blood vessels in the body or in an organ or body part.

# FURTHER RESOURCES

♦

## Bibliography

Angier, Natalie. *Natural Obsessions: Striving to Unlock the Deepest Secrets of the Cancer Cell.* Boston: Mariner Books/Houghton Mifflin, 1999.

Armstrong, Lance, and Sally Jenkins. *It's Not About the Bike: My Journey Back to Life.* New York: Putnam, 2000.

Bazell, Robert. *Her-2: The Making of Herceptin, A Revolutionary Treatment for Breast Cancer.* New York: Random House, 1998.

Diamond, John C. *Because Cowards Get Cancer Too: A Hypochondriac Confronts His Nemesis.* New York: Times Books, 1999.

Dorfman, Elena V. *The C-Word: Teenagers and Their Families Living with Cancer.* Troutdale, OR: NewSage Press, 1998.

Droll et al. "Mortality in Relation to Smoking: 40 years' Observations on Male British Doctors." *British Medical Journal* 309 (1994): 901-911.

Gifford, Rebecca. *Cancer Happens: Coming of Age with Cancer.* Sterling, VA: Capital Books, 2003.

Greaves, Mel. *Cancer: The Evolutionary Legacy.* New York: Oxford University Press, 2002.

Grollman, Earl A. *Straight Talk about Death for Teenagers: How to Cope with Losing Someone You Love.* Boston: Beacon Press, 1993.

Joensuu et. al. "Brief Report: Effect of the Tyrosine Kinase Inhibitor ST1571 in a Patient with a Metastatic Gastrointestinal Stromal Tumor." *New England Journal of Medicine* 344 (2001): 1052-1056.

Sompayrac, Lauren. *How Cancer Works.* Sudbury, MA: Jones and Bartlett, 2003.

Waldholz, Michael. *Curing Cancer: The Story of the Men and Women Unlocking the Secrets of Our Deadliest Illness.* New York: Simon & Schuster, 1997.

Weinberg, Robert A. *One Renegade Cell: How Cancer Begins.* New York: Basic Books, 1998.

————. *Racing to the Beginning of the Road: The Search for the Origin of Cancer.* New York: Harmony Books, 1996.

## Web Sites

**American Cancer Society**
http://www.cancer.org

**Breast Cancer Action**
http://www.thinkbeforeyoupink.org

**CancerQuest**
http://www.cancerquest.org

**Lance Armstrong Foundation**
http://www.livestrong.org

**National Cancer Institute**
http://www.cancer.gov

# INDEX

♦

# ABOUT THE AUTHOR

◆

**PARAIC A. KENNY** is a breast cancer researcher. He was born in Ireland and obtained his bachelor's degree in biochemistry from University College Cork. He began studying mouse models of breast cancer during his doctoral training at the Institute of Cancer Research in London and was awarded a Ph.D. in 2002. Since then, he has worked as a postdoctoral research fellow at Lawrence Berkeley National Laboratory in Berkeley, California, where he has undertaken advanced study of the mechanisms by which human breast cancer cells escape from normal proliferation controls during cancer progression.